DEDICATION

To Casey Hardaker, my partner, lover and my rock. By the time this book is out, we will have been together for 10 years. I thank you for allowing me to chase my dreams and the different sacrifices we have made together. My success is only achieved with you standing beside me and being my backbone. I thank you for never giving up. Love you.

ANNA POLYVIOU

Sweet Street

SHOW-STOPPING SWEET TREATS AND ROCKSTAR DESSERTS

MURDOCH BOOKS

SYDNEY · LONDON

ABOUT 3SOMES

Throughout the book you'll find my wicked 3some recipes. On these pages I take a favourite basic dessert – such as panna cotta or pavlova – and use it in three different ways to show how versatile it can be. You can have lots of fun adding your own special twists. Start with my recipes and use your imagination to make them your own!

Life is about breaking rules, about asking for forgiveness rather than permission, about how we stand out from the rest and what makes us extra-special. When we're told it's impossible then the possible is created.

———————

Sweet Street is a festival that I created back in 2014 at Shangri-La Hotel, Sydney. I wanted to transform the hotel into a festival with my pastry-chef friends from around Australia joining me in showcasing their creations. It's about bringing people together to experience a different world of sweet treats with funky cool beats.

This book has been four years in the making and I have travelled around the world trying to take you to different sweet streets. It's about sweet journeys, from the threesome experience — one recipe presented three different ways — to quick sugar fixes that use items lying around the pantry; old-school classics brought back to look super-cool; and rockstar creations that have featured on TV and have over a hundred steps.

It's about all levels of cooks getting into the kitchen and giving it a go. I don't want you to leave this book on the coffee table or lose it among all the other books on your shelves; I want it to be given as a gift and I want it to get dirty. Use it to impress your family and friends (and yourself) when you learn that spectacular cooking can be easy.

Sharing a dish brings people together. I hope that my sweet streets will cross roads and allow you and your loved ones to create and to eat as one.

THE BEGINNING

An overnight success, some would say, but that's not true: to every story there's always a beginning. A wild child, I was. Not a bad kid, just a little show-off in class. I suppose some things haven't changed.

I applied twice to do an apprenticeship at Hotel Sofitel in Melbourne, but when I got in, instead of taking it seriously, I went off partying. Then I was placed into a team of four in a competition: they needed a pastry chef and they were desperate.

I was doing breakfast in the hotel at the time, so the partying was put on hold and I started to learn pastry on my days off, after work and in breaks. I trained so hard and we came in second place. I felt I had let the team down.

I remember my mother telling me, 'My daughter needs to learn how to lose before she learns how to win.' I understand now what she meant: understanding how it feels to lose and, when you win, to be humble, grateful and respectful.

After that, I won every competition: not because I was the best, but because I was the best organised. I trained like a demon and won the Best Apprentice competition run by Les Toque Blanches in Victoria, Australia. The prize was a scholarship to work anywhere in the world to further my cooking career.

I went to work in London for three years at Claridge's, where I worked under two extraordinary pastry chefs: Julie Sharp, named the UK's Best Pastry Chef 2004 by the Craft Guild of Chefs, and Nick Patterson, who was awarded the same prize four years later. I would sleep in the corner of the training room at the hotel, not going home for weeks on end as I was working, studying and competing. Most prestigiously, I won the Michael Nadell Pastry Trophy, which is how I ended up in Paris doing stints with renowned pastry chef Pierre Hermé.

I came back to Australia after three years of training, developing and growing my skills. My sell-out Dessert Degustation put the Shangri-La on Australia's culinary map. Then in 2015, one of my trademark dishes, a modernist take on the traditional carrot cake, won best dessert in Australia. I was invited onto the TV show *MasterChef Australia* as a guest judge, where I presented the Carrot Cake (see page 126), as well as Anna's Mess (see page 120) and the Firecracker (see page 150).

I've continued winning awards, including the Gault & Millau Pastry Chef of the Year 2016 and Chef of the Year in both 2016 and 2017 from Tourism Accommodation Australia (NSW). In 2017, Channel Nine Australia created a brand new prime-time TV show: *Family Food Fight*, where I was a regular judge and created Anna's Tower of Terror (see page 142). What's next? I want my own TV show, I want to continue writing books and creating experiences for my fans. I hope you enjoy this one.

For me, cooking is about getting people into the kitchen. This chapter has quick and easy desserts that look and taste great, using what's in the pantry, fridge and freezer to create sweet magic that everyone will be talking about.

This trifle is a super-quick, no hassle, impressive creation. It's about sharing and caring. It's always a huge success, plus it's just so easy. Of course, you could make your own jelly and macarons, but in reality not everyone has the time and the skill to do that, so buy these macarons and use packet jelly.

SERVES 8

1 packet of berry-flavoured jelly
   (gelatine dessert)
250 g (9 oz) strawberries, hulled and halved
150 g (5½ oz) raspberries, halved
12 berry-flavoured macarons

Make the jelly mixture according to the directions on the packet and pour it into an 18 cm (7 inch) diameter glass dish. Place in the refrigerator for 1 hour or until set.

Scatter the strawberries and raspberries over the set jelly, followed by the macarons.

QUICK TWIST
Make sure that the jelly is fully set before placing the remaining ingredients on top. Assemble the trifle just before serving. It's easy to change the flavours: just use your imagination!

Why make **macarons** when you can **buy them**? **Cheating to create** has never been so good.

It's all about **mixing old-school and modern flavours:** bombe Alaska with **new-age ice-cream tubs. Da Bomb** is a great way of using up **different ingredients** you have in the **pantry** and the **freezer.**

DA BOMB vs ICE-CREAM TUB PAGES 14–15

DA BOMB

Da Bomb is a cool version of a bombe Alaska, with raspberry ripple ice cream, caramel popcorn ice cream and fudge brownie ice cream all combined into a dome with toasted meringue on the outside, so the different layers are revealed when you cut into it.

Note: You will need a sugar thermometer.

———

SERVES 12

———

500 g (1 lb 2 oz) vanilla ice cream
60 g (2¼ oz) raspberry jam (jelly)
100 g (3½ oz) caramel popcorn
250 g (9 oz) chocolate ice cream
100 g (3½ oz) chocolate brownie, crumbled

ITALIAN MERINGUE
400 g (14 oz) caster (superfine) sugar
7 egg whites

———

Put the vanilla ice cream into the bowl of an electric mixer fitted with the paddle attachment. Beat until it softens.

Divide the mixture in half, putting each half in a separate bowl. Fold the raspberry jam through one of the bowls of ice cream and the popcorn through the other. Transfer to the freezer.

Put the chocolate ice cream into the bowl of an electric mixer fitted with the paddle attachment. Beat until it softens and fold in the brownie crumble. Transfer the chocolate ice cream to the freezer.

To assemble, line a 22 cm (8½ inch) diameter stainless steel bowl with plastic wrap, ensuring that it hangs over the edge of the bowl.

Remove the vanilla raspberry ice cream from the freezer and spoon the mixture into the prepared bowl. Smooth it out to make an even layer in the base of the bowl. Freeze until firm. Repeat with the popcorn ice cream and freeze until firm. Finally,

repeat with the chocolate fudge mixture and return to the freezer for 1–2 hours while you make the Italian meringue.

Put the sugar in a small saucepan with just enough water to make a thick slurry – about 100 ml (3½ fl oz) – and cook until the syrup is 121°C (250°F) on a sugar thermometer.

When the syrup is about 118°C (244°F), whisk the egg whites in an electric mixer fitted with the whisk attachment, until soft peaks form.

Turn the mixer to low speed and slowly pour the hot syrup into the egg whites. Increase the speed to high and whisk until the mixture has cooled to just warm and is thick and glossy.

To assemble, turn the frozen ice cream layers out onto a serving platter. Put the meringue into a piping (icing) bag with a size 15 plain nozzle and pipe it in a thick layer all over the ice cream, starting from the base. If you like you can toast the meringue with a blowtorch, being careful not to burn it, or just leave it untoasted.

———

QUICK TWIST
Change up the flavours, using up leftover ice cream and whatever else is in the pantry. You can add a sponge-cake layer on the top of the bowl (it becomes the base of the bombe): simply buy a ready-made cake and cut it to the size you require.

I love eating ice cream in bed while watching a movie and, when I stay in hotels for work or pleasure, I like to replicate that cool, comfy feeling. I put ice cream in a tub on my room-service menu and people go nuts!

SERVES 2

100 g (3½ oz) honeycomb (sponge candy)
100 g (3½ oz) Anzac biscuits (rolled oats and
    honey cookies)
50 g (1¾ oz) caramel popcorn
500 g (1 lb 2 oz) tub of salted caramel ice cream

Break the honeycomb and biscuits into small pieces. Combine with the popcorn in a medium bowl.

Put the ice cream in the bowl of an electric mixer fitted with the paddle attachment and beat until softened. Remove from the machine and fold in half of the honeycomb mixture. Return the ice cream to the tub and pile the remaining honeycomb mixture on top.

QUICK TWIST
If you can't find salted caramel ice cream, just buy caramel ice cream and stir through some sea salt.

One of my **favourite things** to eat is **ice cream** straight out of the tub!

SALTED CARAMEL ICE-CREAM TUB

MILK 'N' COOKIES PAGE 18

2 EASY CHOCOLATE MOUSSE

Way too easy: just water and chocolate whisked together and finished with a pinch of sea salt to take the bitterness out of the chocolate.

SERVES 8

400 g (14 oz) dark chocolate (70%),
    chopped or buttons
sea salt, to serve

Put the chocolate into a heatproof bowl.

In a small saucepan, bring 350 ml (12 fl oz) of water to the boil over high heat. Remove from the heat and gradually pour the water over the chocolate, stirring constantly until all of the chocolate has dissolved and the liquid is smooth and shiny.

Cover the surface with plastic wrap. Transfer to the refrigerator and allow to cool to 34°C (93°F).

Transfer the cooled liquid to the bowl of an electric mixer fitted with the whisk attachment. Whisk on high speed for 3–5 minutes until it reaches a thick mousse consistency. Chill in the refrigerator for 1–2 hours until firm enough to quenelle.

To serve, dip a metal dessertspoon into hot water and use it to form quenelles. Place the quenelles onto serving plates and sprinkle with a pinch of sea salt.

QUICK TWIST
This is an ideal quicky dessert for people with dietary issues: vegans love this!

MILK 'N' COOKIES

Rum balls are a simple and classic party treat. Whenever I put them on the menu, I spend more time eating them than making them! I've left the rum out completely so these are just the basics: arrowroot biscuits and let's not forget the yummy sweetened condensed milk.

MAKES 40

250 g (9 oz/1 packet) arrowroot biscuits
    (cookies), crushed
395 g (13¾ oz) tin sweetened condensed milk
250 g (9 oz) desiccated (shredded) coconut
75 g (2¾ oz/⅔ cup) cocoa powder
extra coconut and chocolate sprinkles
    for rolling

Put the crushed biscuits, condensed milk, coconut and cocoa powder in the bowl of an electric mixer fitted with the paddle attachment. Beat on medium speed for 2–3 minutes until well combined.

Use your hands to roll tablespoons of the mixture into balls. Spread the extra coconut and the chocolate sprinkles on separate trays and roll the balls in the coconut or chocolate sprinkles to coat. Refrigerate for 30–60 minutes until firm.

Cut foil into 5 cm (2 inch) squares and cut coloured cellophane into 8 cm (3¼ inch) squares. Wrap each ball in foil and cellophane and twist the top of each wrapper to seal.

QUICK TWIST
These are very addictive: try not to pop too many in your mouth while you're wrapping them.

RAZZLE B BASIL SNOW CONE

Ideal for summer, this quick and refreshing dessert is a different way to present granita: instead of having it in a glass, it's in a cone. Usually icy treats are full of sugar syrup, but this is mainly fruit purées and juices.

———————

SERVES 6

———————

50 g (1¾ oz) caster (superfine) sugar
150 ml (5 fl oz) passionfruit purée (see glossary)
150 ml (5 fl oz) orange juice
¼ bunch of basil, washed and coarsely chopped

———————

Put the caster sugar in a small saucepan with 75 ml (2¼ fl oz) of water bring to a simmer over medium heat. Meanwhile, mix together the orange juice and passionfruit purée in a medium bowl.

When the sugar has dissolved, remove the syrup from the heat and add the basil. Set aside for 1 hour to allow the flavour to infuse. Strain, then stir in the orange and passionfruit mixture.

Pour the liquid into a wide freezer-proof dish and put it in the freezer until it freezes solid. Scrape the mixture with a fork and then return the dish to the freezer. Repeat the scraping every 30 minutes until all the mixture is turned into icy flakes.

Scoop the granita into waxed paper cones, hand them out and you'll be the life of the party.

———————

QUICK TWIST
Add some vodka to the granita once it's been made (for adults only). You can buy the paper cones from party supply stores. Change the flavour around with seasonal fruit: you might need to experiment with the quantities and freezing time but this is a good base recipe.

CASEY'S CHOC-DIPPED STRAWBERRIES

My partner just rocks: her cooking is simple yet tasty. One evening she wanted something sweet, so she went to the pantry and found some dark chocolate and a punnet of strawberries in the fridge. Good for you and a little bit naughty: she went ahead and dipped them and ate them.

———————

SERVES 4

———————

150 g (5½ oz) good-quality dark chocolate, chopped or buttons
250 g (9 oz) strawberries, washed and dried only (don't hull them)

———————

Line a baking tray with baking paper and set aside.

Put the chocolate into a microwave-proof bowl, and heat the chocolate in 40-second bursts, stirring after each one, until the chocolate has completely melted. This should take about 3–4 minutes.

Hold the strawberry by the green leafy end and dip it into the chocolate.

Gently wipe the strawberry on the side of the bowl to remove excess chocolate.

Place the strawberry on the prepared tray and repeat with the remaining strawberries. Put the tray in the refrigerator for about 15–20 minutes, until the chocolate has set.

———————

QUICK TWIST
If you're in a hurry to eat the chocolate-dipped strawberries, pop the tray in the freezer for 5–10 minutes and they'll be ready to go. Dip other fruit — such as bananas, grapes and pineapple — in chocolate for different tastes. Make sure not to overheat the chocolate or it will take longer to set.

The following three recipes are different examples of what you can do with breakfast bakery leftovers: turn croissants into sweet treats or danishes into bread-and-butter puddings. I dislike wastage and love to cross food over to another usage. I use these items on the buffet at work: the croissants for breakfast and the pudding for dinner. Both do very well!

ALMOND AND APPLE CROISSANTS

SERVES 10

10 croissants
50 g (1¾ oz/½ cup) flaked almonds
250 g (9 oz) tinned chopped apples
icing (confectioners') sugar, for the finishing touches

ALMOND FRANGIPANE
100 g (3½ oz) unsalted butter, softened
100 g (3½ oz) icing (confectioners') sugar
100 g (3½ oz/1 cup) almond meal
1 egg

RUM SYRUP
250 g (9 oz) caster (superfine) sugar
50 ml (1¾ fl oz) dark rum

To make the frangipane, use an electric mixer fitted with the paddle attachment to beat the butter and icing sugar on medium speed for 2–3 minutes until light and fluffy. Turn off the mixer and scrape down the side of the bowl.

Return to medium speed and add the almond meal and the egg, beating until combined. Turn the mixer off and scrape down the side of the bowl.

Return to medium speed for a final stir until it is well combined. Cover the surface of the mixture with plastic wrap and transfer the bowl to the refrigerator to rest for at least 1 hour.

Meanwhile, make the rum syrup. Combine the sugar and rum with 400 ml (14 fl oz) of water in a medium saucepan over high heat and bring to the boil. Remove from the heat and keep warm until needed.

To assemble, preheat the oven to 180°C (350°F). Line a baking tray with baking paper.

Use a size 12 plain piping nozzle to make a hole in the base of each croissant. Dip the croissant in the warm rum syrup, making sure to submerge them completely.

Lay the croissants on a wire rack and allow excess syrup to drip off. Fill a piping (icing) bag fitted with a size 12 plain nozzle three-quarters full with almond frangipane.

Spoon a tablespoon of tinned apple into each croissant, then pipe a teaspoon of almond frangipane on top and scatter the flaked almonds over the top.

Transfer the croissants to the prepared tray. Bake for 20–25 minutes until the croissants are golden brown. Remove from the oven and dust with icing sugar to serve.

QUICK TWIST
The syrup and frangipane can be made up to 5 days in advance and stored in an airtight container in the refrigerator. Alternatively assemble the croissants and freeze them on the tray until you are ready to bake them.

MIXED BERRY AND VANILLA CROISSANTS

SERVES 10

300 g (10½ oz) caster (superfine) sugar
10 croissants
300 g (10½ oz) PUMP UP ... THE JAM (see page 232)
1 quantity VANILLA PASTRY CRÈME (see page 233)

In a small saucepan, stir together 400 ml (14 fl oz) of water and the sugar, then bring to the boil over high heat. Remove from the heat and transfer the syrup to a medium bowl to cool slightly.

Preheat the oven to 160°C (315°F). Line a baking tray with baking paper and set it aside. Use a plain size 8 piping (icing) nozzle to make a small hole in the bottom of each croissant.

Fill a piping (icing) bag fitted with the size 8 nozzle with the jam and pipe about 30 g (1 oz) of jam into each croissant.

Fill a clean piping bag fitted with a size 8 nozzle with the vanilla pastry crème. Pipe the pastry cream into each croissant until it is completely full but not bursting.

Dip each croissant into the sugar syrup and then lay it on a wire rack with a tray underneath to allow excess syrup to drip off.

Transfer the croissants to the prepared baking tray, leaving a 3 cm (1 ¼ inch) space between them. Bake for 20–25 minutes or until crisp.

Remove from the oven and cool slightly on the tray.

QUICK TWIST
As with many things, if you have made too much, just freeze it and bring it out when required. Make sure the sugar syrup is warm so it is absorbed into the croissant when soaking.

JAMMING WITH DANISH

SERVES 8

200 ml (7 fl oz) milk
1 vanilla bean, split and seeds scraped
3 eggs
50 g (1¾ oz) caster (superfine) sugar
10 danishes, chopped into 2 cm (¾ inch) pieces
100 g (3½ oz) PUMP UP ... THE JAM (see page 232)
100 ml (3½ fl oz) BRUSH ME PRETTY (see page 232)

Preheat the oven to 150°C (300°F).

Combine the milk, vanilla bean and seeds in a small saucepan over medium heat.

Whisk together the eggs and caster sugar in a stainless steel bowl until completely combined.

When the milk has come to the boil, remove from the heat and pour the hot liquid into the egg mixture. Whisk until well combined and pass through a fine sieve into a large jug.

Place eight espresso cups in a baking dish and divide half of the chopped danish evenly among the cups.

Divide half the jam between the cups and pour the custard mixture into the cups until the danish is just covered. Fill the cups with the remaining danish and then the remaining custard mixture, then add a teaspoon of jam on the top of each one.

Bake for 15–20 minutes until no liquid comes up when the you push down on the pudding. Remove from the oven and brush with warm nappage.

QUICK TWIST
I tend to make this in a large dish at home, but I've also made individual puddings in espresso cups, which are pretty and cute. Bread-and-butter pudding was a poor person's dessert when there was leftover bread; I'm using leftover danish to create something even more tasty than the original product. Serve warm with a custard sauce. Use danish, croissants or even pain au chocolat.

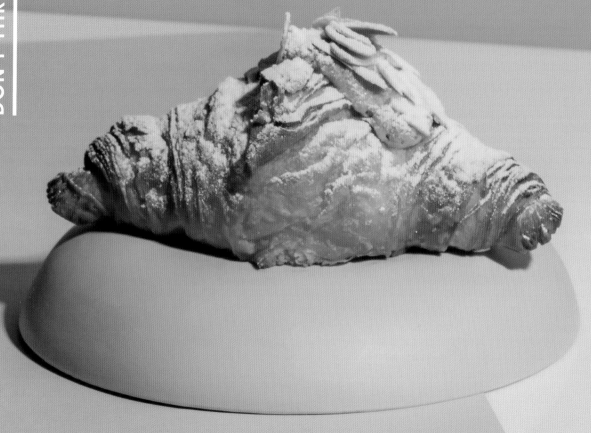

I love going to the movies: it's one of my favourite things to do, and part of the experience is all the food that you eat while you watch. Movie food treats include popcorn, choc-malt balls, chips and jelly sweets.

SERVES 6

20 g (¾ oz) packet salted potato chips (crisps)
40 g (1½ oz) caramel popcorn
40 g (1½ oz) raspberry jelly lollies (jelly candy)
80 g (2¾ oz) honeycomb (sponge candy)
350 g (12 oz) milk chocolate, melted in 30-second
     bursts in the microwave

Spray a 24 x 30 x 5 cm (9½ x 12 x 2 inch) baking tin with canola oil and line it with baking paper.

In a medium bowl, mix together all of the ingredients except the chocolate.

Melt the chocolate and fold half of the mixture through the chocolate, then spread it evenly on the prepared tray.

Scatter the rest of the mixture on top, once again making sure it is spread evenly.

Transfer to the refrigerator for 15–20 minutes, until set. Slide the whole piece onto a work surface with baking paper underneath.

Use a small hammer or a rolling pin to smash the chocolate into bite-size pieces.

QUICK TWIST
Use your favourite movie snacks, but taste everything together before getting overly creative.

I just throw all my **fave flavours** together into a **popcorn box** and get an **extra surprise** every time my hand goes **to my mouth!**

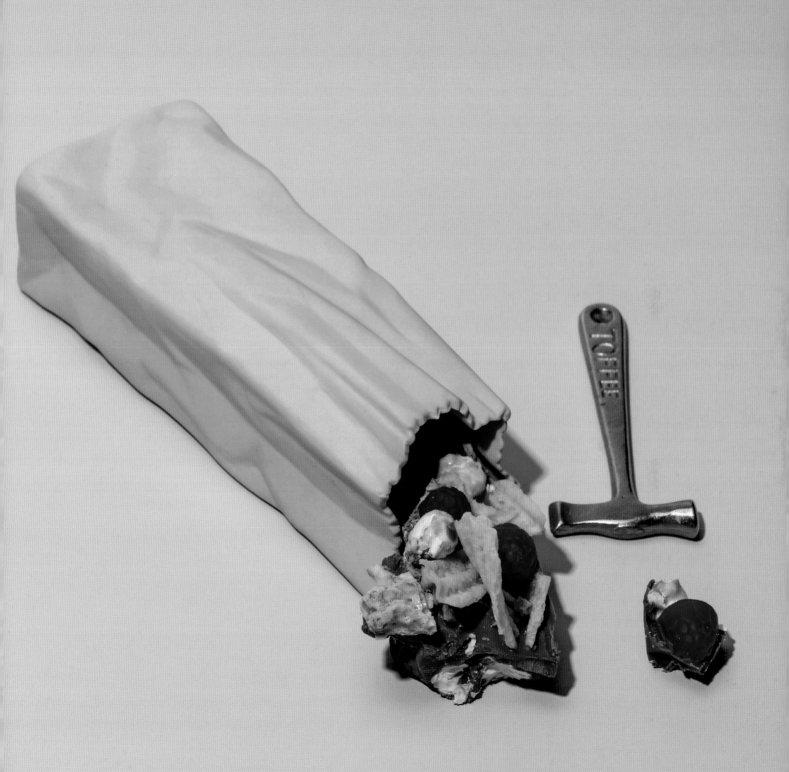

CHERRY ON TOP

I grew up with this quick cake recipe: Mum learned it from a lady at work and ended up making it for every occasion. For birthdays, kitchen teas, a Sunday family lunch: the occasion didn't matter. It's just whipped cream and chocolate biscuits, with a cherry on top to finish it.

SERVES 6

500 ml (17 fl oz/2 cups) pure (pouring) cream (35% fat)
20 g (¾ oz) icing (confectioners') sugar
1 teaspoon vanilla paste
1 packet chocolate-flavoured biscuits (cookies)
6 glacé cherries with stems

Combine the cream, icing sugar and vanilla paste in the bowl of an electric mixer fitted with the whisk attachment. Whisk until semifirm.

Lay one biscuit down on a tray and put 1 tablespoon of whipped cream on top. Put another biscuit on top of the first one and top with whipped cream. Continue to make a stack of four biscuits and cream.

Dollop the cream on top of the last biscuit.

Finish the creation with a cherry on top, then refrigerate for 1–2 hours before serving to allow the cream to soak into the biscuits

QUICK TWIST
You can make this as a big cake in a loaf (bar) or round tin, and use chocolate sprinkles or anything you like. Blitz any remaining biscuits in a food processor and sprinkle the crumbs on.

Simple things in life are often **the best:** **slip** a biscuit on a tray, **slop** on some cream and **slap a cherry on top!**

I'm a massive fan of soufflés and normally I would make one with a pastry crème base, which tends to take a little longer but also holds the shape when it comes out of the oven. This recipe is a lot quicker, although the holding time isn't long: you only have a few seconds before it starts collapsing.

SERVES 8

---

100 g (3½ oz) unsalted butter, softened, for moulds
200 g (7 oz) caster (superfine) sugar, plus 50 g
   (1¾ oz) extra for moulds
8 eggs, separated
50 ml (1¾ fl oz) lemonade (lemon-flavoured soda)
100 ml (3½ fl oz) lemon juice
zest of 1 lemon
1 tablespoon icing (confectioners') sugar, for dusting

Preheat the oven to 200°C (400°F). Lightly grease eight tall ovenproof dishes with the softened butter. Use a pastry brush to brush the butter upwards as this will help the soufflé to rise.

Sprinkle the extra caster sugar into a greased dish and turn it in your hand to coat the inside all over with the sugar, before pouring out the loose sugar. Repeat this with the remaining dishes and stand them on a baking tray.

To make the soufflé, put the egg whites in the bowl of an electric mixer fitted with the whisk attachment. Whisk on high speed until firm peaks form. Add half of the caster sugar and continue mixing until very stiff peaks form. Transfer to another bowl and set aside.

Put the egg yolks and remaining sugar in the bowl of the electric mixer and whisk until pale and creamy. Remove the bowl from the mixer and gently fold in the lemonade and the lemon juice until combined.

Gently fold through the egg whites and lemon zest, in stages so it doesn't collapse, working slowly until all combined. Scoop the mixture evenly into the soufflé dishes on the tray.

Bake for 12–15 minutes, or until well risen: the soufflé will form a crust and have a slight golden colour.

Remove from the oven, dust with icing sugar and serve immediately.

QUICK TWIST

Make sure that the oven is hot or the soufflés won't rise; don't open the door or they will collapse; and serve immediately or they will collapse before they get to the table. There isn't really anything to hold the soufflés together so they will deflate if not served straight away.

DEFLATED... LEMONADE SOUFFLÉ PAGE 31

ESPRESSO TIRAMISU

Served in a martini glass, an espresso tiramisu creates a little bit of theatre when you put it together in front of your guests.

SERVES 6

100 g (3½ oz) savoiardi (lady fingers) halved
    lengthways then cut in thirds crossways
125 ml (4 fl oz/½ cup) espresso coffee
2 tablespoons coffee-flavoured liqueur,
    such as Kahlua
1 tablespoon vodka
crushed ice
200 g (7 oz) mascarpone
100 ml (3½ fl oz) pure (pouring) cream (35% fat),
    lightly whipped
1 tablespoon icing (confectioners') sugar, sifted
30 g (1 oz) chocolate, to be grated during serving

Divide the savoiardi between 6 martini glasses and pour the espresso coffee over the top.

Combine the liqueur, vodka and crushed ice in a cocktail shaker and shake for 1 minute to chill the alcohol. Strain and pour 1 tablespoon of the liquid into each martini glass.

Put the mascarpone, cream and icing sugar into a small bowl. Use a tablespoon to beat them together until combined, then spoon the mixture evenly over the sponge fingers.

Sprinkle finely grated chocolate on top of the whipped mascarpone cream and serve.

HIGHLIGHTS

This dessert is most dramatic when prepared on the spot, whether in front of guests at home or in a restaurant. It's a fun, interactive creation for everyone to be involved in. Try switching the savoiardi with sponge cake and adding strawberries.

This quick dessert is **super-easy**, fun and a little **naughty** if you add some **alcohol.**

Take a basic cheesecake and add imagination to turn it into three different fun sweets. Pile on fresh fruit, plate up a sweet cheesy gnocchi or whip up some push, push, push-it pops.

Everyone loves cheesecake; it's one of those sweet creations that's always welcome at a dinner party. This version, with fresh berries, is simple and yet super-tasty.

SERVES 8–12

40 g (1½ oz) unsalted butter, melted
½ vanilla bean, seeds scraped
120 g (4¼ oz) digestive biscuits (plain sweet cookies), blitzed in a food processor

CHEESECAKE MIXTURE
600 g (1 lb 5 oz) cream cheese
180 g (6¼ oz) caster (superfine) sugar
2 eggs
20 g (¾ oz) white chocolate, melted
½ vanilla bean, split and seeds scraped

TO ASSEMBLE
125 g (4½ oz) strawberries, hulled and quartered
75 g (2¾ oz) raspberries, halved
110 g (3¾ oz) blackberries, halved
BRUSH ME PRETTY nappage (see page 232)
baby basil leaves

Line an 18–20 cm (7–8 inch) springform cake tin with baking paper.

In a small saucepan, bring the butter and vanilla bean and seeds to the boil. Keep cooking for about 3–5 minutes until the butter has a nutty smell to it and has coloured slightly. Remove from the stove and discard the vanilla bean.

Mix together the biscuits and the vanilla butter until well combined.

Spoon the biscuit mixture into the prepared tin, pressing down so the base is covered evenly. Refrigerate until ready to use.

Preheat the oven to 165°C (320°F).

In an electric mixer fitted with the paddle attachment, beat the cream cheese until smooth. Scrape down the side of the bowl, then add the sugar and beat until well combined.

With the mixer on slow speed, add the eggs one at a time, beating until well combined. Add the melted chocolate and the vanilla seeds.

Pour the cheesecake mixture on top of the biscuit base, using a spatula to make sure it is smooth and flat.

Bake for 30 minutes until almost firm: check whether it is cooked by tapping the side of the tin; if it wobbles too much, return it to the oven for a further 5 minutes.

Increase the oven temperature to 250°C (500°F) and cook the cheesecake for a further 2–3 minutes, until golden. Remove from the oven and set aside to cool in the tin.

To assemble, arrange the berries on top of the cheesecake. Warm the nappage and use a pastry brush to lightly glaze the berries. Finish off the cake by garnishing with baby basil leaves.

3SOME TWIST
Use any in-season fruit as a topping. Make sure you don't undercook the cheesecake, otherwise it runs when you cut into it; on the other hand, you don't want to overcook it or it will be grainy, browned and cracked. You can keep it in the freezer for 1–2 weeks, so it's a great dessert to make in advance.

BERRIED PUSH POPS

At my very first cooking demo I was going to make a cheesecake push pop, but I needed it to be more exciting. I added a fairy floss (candy floss) machine and had my personal DJ play 'Push It' by Salt-N-Pepa while I was doing my demo. It was a HUGE hit. That is how I started having a DJ for my cooking demos: they're not your average demo, a little more like a concert.

MAKES 15 PUSH POPS

1 quantity of CHEESECAKE MIXTURE (see page 39)

STRAWBERRY JELLY (gelatine dessert)
250 g (9 oz) strawberries, hulled
55 g (2 oz/¼ cup) caster (superfine) sugar
2 sheets titanium-strength gelatine, softened in cold water

TO ASSEMBLE
300 g (10½ oz) digestive biscuits (plain sweet cookies), blitzed in a food processor
250 g (9 oz) strawberries, hulled and quartered
150 g (5½ oz) raspberries, halved
220 g (8 oz) blackberries, halved
150 g (5½ oz) blueberries, halved
1 packet ready-made fairy floss (candy floss)

Preheat the oven to 165°C (320°F). Grease and line an 18 cm (7 inch) square or round cake tin.

In an electric mixer fitted with the paddle attachment, beat the cream cheese until smooth. Scrape down the side of the bowl, then add the sugar and beat well combined.

With the mixer on slow speed, add the eggs one at a time, beating until well combined. Add the melted chocolate and the vanilla seeds.

Pour the mixture into the prepared cake tin, making sure it is smooth and flat.

Bake for 30 minutes until almost firm: check whether it is cooked by tapping the side of the tin;

if it wobbles too much, return it to the oven for a further 5 minutes. Set aside to cool in the tin until needed for assembly.

To make the jelly, toss the strawberries in the sugar, put them in a bowl and set aside overnight so the juices come out of the strawberries. Strain the strawberries and juice, but do not press the strawberries through the sieve. Reserve the liquid (consommé) and save the strawberries to add to your breakfast.

In a small saucepan, bring 200 ml (7 fl oz) of the strawberry juice and 50 ml (1¾ fl oz) of water to the boil, then squeeze excess liquid out of the softened gelatine and stir the gelatine through the juice until completely dissolved. Strain and cool before use.

Pour 1 tablespoon of jelly mixture into each push pop mould and put them in the refrigerator to set. Make sure the moulds are upright.

When the jelly has set, cut the baked cheesecake into chunks and put it in the bowl of an electric mixer fitted with the paddle attachment. Beat the cheesecake on medium to high speed until completely smooth.

Transfer the cheesecake to a piping (icing) bag fitted with a size 12 nozzle. Pipe the cheesecake into each push pop mould on top of the jelly until halfway up the side, followed by a spoonful of biscuit crumbs.

Top each push pop with mixed berries and a small amount of fairy floss.

Note: You can buy push pop moulds online or from cake decorating and party supply stores.

3SOME TWIST

Freeze the consommé and thaw it out to make the jelly — drink the leftovers with Champagne. The cheesecake can be frozen. For a gluten-free dessert, leave out the biscuits. It's okay to use strawberry jelly from a packet instead of making your own.

Turn a savoury dish – cheese gnocchi – around to make a fun dessert. The edible flowers are like a mini salad on top; the sweet biscuit crumbs replace breadcrumbs and you serve it with fruit instead of vegetables.

SERVES 8

1 quantity CHEESECAKE MIXTURE (see page 39)
1 handful edible flowers

POACHED STONE FRUIT
400 g (14 oz) caster (superfine) sugar
1 vanilla bean, split and seeds scraped
2 white peaches, stones removed, thinly sliced
   (use a mandolin if you have one)
4 yellow peaches, stones removed, cut into 10 thin
   wedges each

BISCUIT CRUMBS
1 vanilla bean, split and seeds scraped
40 g (1½ oz) unsalted butter, at room temperature
120 g (4¼ oz) digestive biscuits (plain sweet cookies)

Preheat the oven to 165°C (320°F). Line the bottom of an 18 cm (7 inch) square or round cake tin with baking paper and then foil. Grease the tin and stand it on a baking tray. Set aside.

In an electric mixer fitted with the paddle attachment, beat the cream cheese until smooth.

When the mixture is smooth, scrape down the side, add the sugar and beat until combined.

Turn the electric mixer off and scrape down the side of the bowl, then with the mixer on slow speed add the eggs one at a time, making sure the first egg is completely combined before adding the next one.

Reduce the speed to medium and add the melted chocolate and the vanilla seeds.

Pour the mixture into the prepared tin.

Bake in the oven for 25–30 minutes, then check it by tapping it gently: it will wobble slightly. If it's too wobbly bake for a further 5 minutes. Remove the cake from the oven and set aside to cool.

Once the cheesecake has cooled, transfer it to an electric mixer fitted with the paddle attachment and beat the cheesecake until it is just softened and there are no lumps.

Meanwhile, line a baking tray with baking paper. If you like, you can rule lines on the back of the baking paper to use as a guide for piping the gnocchi mixture. Using a plain size 15 piping (icing) nozzle, pipe lines of the mixture across the lined baking paper and put it in the freezer for at least 30 minutes until frozen.

Meanwhile, poach the fruit: in a medium saucepan, bring the sugar and the vanilla seeds with 400 ml (14 fl oz) water to the boil over medium heat.

Lay the sliced fruit on a tray.

When the sugar syrup is ready, remove from the heat and pour over the slices of fruit. Cover the surface with plastic wrap and set aside to cool in the refrigerator.

Make biscuit crumbs. In a small saucepan, combine the vanilla bean and seeds with the butter and bring it to the boil. Keep cooking until the butter has coloured slightly and has a nutty smell. Once it has boiled, remove from the heat and discard the vanilla pod.

Put the biscuits in a food processor and process to make coarse crumbs. Tip into a bowl.

Pour the butter mixture over the biscuit crumbs and mix until well combined. Refrigerate until needed.

To assemble, remove the cheesecake gnocchi from the freezer and cut into 3 cm (1¼ inch) pieces. Place 10 gnocchi pieces on each plate.

Remove the fruit slices from the sugar syrup and place on paper towel to drain the excess syrup. Arrange the slices of stone fruit evenly among the eight plates. Spoon the biscuit crumbs evenly among the plates.

Drizzle with the vanilla sugar syrup and then garnish with the edible flowers.

3SOME TWIST
Make sure the cheesecake is frozen, otherwise it will be too soft and difficult to handle to place on the plate.

I'm old-school at heart:
I love soufflés, crepes,
crème brûlées and the rest.
This chapter is about
reintroducing those classic
sweets with a modern, cool
twist. As we all know, the
classics always come back:
childhood memories and
culinary ones too.

How I love eating this traditional dessert: cold, warm or hot; any style is fine with me. You can serve it in the dish, but I like it turned out so you can see the curd on top. This was part of a dessert I created that helped get a restaurant awarded a chef's hat. The plate had an additional four elements on it, but the review was all about the lemon delicious: they forgot to mention anything else.

SERVES 8

50 g (1¾ oz) unsalted butter, at room temperature
165 g (5¾ oz/¾ cup) caster (superfine) sugar, 100 g (3½ oz) extra for coating dishes
zest of 1 lemon
50 ml (1¾ fl oz) passionfruit juice, warmed
40 g (1½ oz) plain (all-purpose) flour, sifted
1 teaspoon baking powder
2 eggs, separated, whites whisked to soft peaks
110 ml (3¾ fl oz) milk

VANILLA CRÈME ANGLAISE
100 ml (3½ fl oz) milk
100 ml (3½ fl oz) thickened (whipping) cream
1 vanilla bean, split and seeds scraped
2 egg yolks
70 g (2½ oz) caster (superfine) sugar

To make the vanilla crème anglaise, put the milk, cream and vanilla bean in a small saucepan and bring it to the boil over medium heat.

In a small bowl, whisk together the egg yolks and sugar. When the milk mixture has come to a boil, pour half onto the egg mixture and whisk well.

Pour the mixture back into the saucepan and return to medium heat. Heat to 84°C (183°F) using a thermometer, or until it thickly coats the back of a spoon, stirring constantly.

Remove from the heat and strain into a medium bowl. Place the bowl in a bath of iced water to cool, stirring constantly. When cooled, lay plastic wrap on the surface to prevent a skin forming and transfer the bowl to the refrigerator until ready to serve.

To make the lemon delicious, preheat the oven to 150°C (300°F). Spray two 13 cm (5 inch) diameter round ovenproof dishes with oil and sprinkle the inside with sugar until coated. Tap out any excess.

In an electric mixer fitted with the paddle attachment, beat the butter and sugar for 3–4 minutes on high speed, until light and fluffy.

Reduce the speed to medium and add the lemon zest. Turn the mixer off and scrape down the side of the bowl.

Return the speed to low and gradually add the warm passionfruit juice. Add the sifted flour and baking powder, alternating with the egg yolks. Turn the mixer off again and scrape down the side of the bowl.

Return the speed to low and slowly add the cold milk, until all is combined. Remove from the mixer and fold through the beaten egg whites until all are combined.

Divide the mixture between the prepared dishes, pouring it in until the dishes are three-quarters full.

Stand the dishes in a larger baking dish. Add enough water to come halfway up the sides of the pudding dishes.

Bake for 60 minutes, or until the mixture comes away from the sides of the dishes.

Allow to cool in the dishes. Carefully turn the puddings out of the dishes onto serving plates and serve with the vanilla crème anglaise.

COOL TWIST
Make it in advance and chill it, then reheat it in the microwave for a few seconds (take it out of the fridge and allow it to reach room temperature first). The crème anglaise is a favourite of mine. I love to drink it on its own, and I use leftovers to make ice cream when I've made too much.

Long churros, freshly fried, will give you tingles in the tummy. These days you can buy individual ones, sometimes already filled so you don't have to dip them. This recipe is for dip-and-eat churros, so you can add as much sauce as you like.

SERVES 6

---

180 ml (6 fl oz/¾ cup) milk
2 teaspoons caster (superfine) sugar
60 g (2¼ oz) unsalted butter, at room temperature
150 g (5½ oz/1 cup) plain (all-purpose) flour
2 eggs
canola oil, for deep-frying

CINNAMON SUGAR
110 g (3¾ oz/½ cup) caster (superfine) sugar
1 teaspoon ground cinnamon

To make the cinnamon sugar, combine the sugar and cinnamon in a bowl and set aside.

Put the milk, sugar and butter in a small saucepan with a pinch of salt and bring to the boil. Remove from the heat and stir in the flour.

Return to the heat and stir constantly for about 3–5 minutes until the flour has incorporated into the liquid, the mixture comes away from the sides and is glossy.

Transfer the mixture into an electric mixer fitted with the paddle attachment and beat on medium speed for 2 minutes to allow the mixture to cool down slightly.

Add the eggs gradually until the mixture comes away from the side, is glossy and all eggs have been incorporated.

Transfer the mixture to a piping (icing) bag fitted with a star nozzle size 8.

Heat a deep-fryer to 175°C (345°F). If you don't have a deep-fryer, heat the oil in a large, deep-sided saucepan until a cube of bread dropped into the oil turns golden brown in 15–20 seconds.

Working in batches, carefully pipe 15 cm (6 inch) lengths of the pastry directly into the oil. Fry for 3–4 minutes until golden brown. Remove from the deep-fryer and drain the excess oil on paper towel. Toss the hot churros in the cinnamon sugar and serve with your favourite sweet dipping sauce.

SALTED CARAMEL DIPPING SAUCE
My favourite sauce is salted caramel (dulce de leche). Buy it ready-made, or make your own: submerge a 375 g (13 oz) tin of sweetened condensed milk in a medium saucepan of simmering water and simmer for 4 hours. Ensure that the water always covers the tin and top it up with boiling water if necessary. Allow the tin to cool completely before opening it to serve the sauce. Stir in a pinch of sea salt.

COOL TWIST
Pipe the churros onto a tray lined with baking paper and freeze them. Once they are frozen, transfer them to an airtight container and keep frozen until ready to use. You can put the frozen churros straight into the deep-fryer, as they hold their shape better.

Churros come in all **shapes and sizes** these days. From round for **ice-cream sandwiches** to mini for canapés. **I prefer them long...**

I remember eating finger buns as a kid at primary school: they were always buttered and we would place barbecue-flavoured savoury biscuits in them. That just made them extra tasty!

SERVES 8

---

200 g (7 oz/1⅓ cups) plain (all-purpose) flour, plus extra for kneading
30 g (1 oz) caster (superfine) sugar
5 g (⅛ oz) fresh yeast
20 g (¾ oz) unsalted butter, at room temperature
150 ml (5 fl oz) milk
1 tablespoon vegetable oil

SUGAR MILK WASH
100 g (3½ oz) caster (superfine) sugar
50 ml (1¾ fl oz) milk

COLOURED ICING
300 g (10½ oz) icing (confectioners') sugar, sifted
a few drops of pink food colouring
20 g (¾ oz/¼ cup) shredded coconut

Put the flour, sugar and yeast and a pinch of salt in the bowl of an electric mixer fitted with the hook attachment. Try to keep the yeast and the salt separate until you start mixing.

In a small saucepan, heat the butter and milk over low heat, just until the butter has melted and the milk is warm.

Pour the milk mixture into the flour and mix for 5 minutes until everything comes together. The dough should be smooth and form into a ball.

Grease a large bowl with half the vegetable oil and transfer the dough. Brush with the remaining vegetable oil and cover with plastic wrap. Set aside in a warm area for 1–2 hours until doubled in size.

Lightly grease a tray with cooking spray. Turn the dough out of the bowl onto a lightly floured work surface and divide into eight 50 g (1¾ oz) pieces. Knead into long finger-shaped buns.

Cover with plastic wrap. Allow to prove (rise) again for a further 40–60 minutes until risen and fluffy.

Meanwhile, preheat the oven to 180°C (350°F). Brush the tops of the risen buns lightly with milk and bake for 15–20 minutes until golden brown.

To make the sugar milk wash, put the sugar and milk in a small saucepan with 60 ml (2 fl oz/¼ cup) of water, and bring it to the boil over medium heat. Remove from the heat and allow to cool.

Remove the buns from the oven and brush with sugar milk wash while still warm, then set aside to cool.

To make the icing, put the icing sugar and 2 tablespoons of water in the bowl of an electric mixer fitted with the whisk attachment. Whisk on low speed until completely combined and smooth.

Reduce the speed to low and add food colouring, a drop at a time, until you have the desired shade. Pour the icing into a shallow bowl or plate to make it easier to dip the buns. Put the coconut in a similar bowl or plate.

Dip the tops of the finger buns into the icing and allow the excess icing to drip off, then dip the iced bun into the coconut.

COOL TWIST
Have fun with this recipe. You can finish the buns with hundreds and thousands (nonpareils) or even change the colour of the icing. I have filled them with everything from jam to flavoured whipped cream, but do try the barbecue-flavoured savoury biscuits, an Aussie favourite of mine.

I love the theatre behind crepes suzette: having it made at the table by a waiter (called 'gueridon service') and then lighting it up with the alcohol and seeing everyone get excited. The alcohol evaporates with the heat, so children can eat the dish too.

SERVES 8

40 g (1½ oz) caster (superfine) sugar
125 g (4½ oz) plain (all-purpose) flour, sifted
225 ml (7¾ fl oz) milk
2 eggs
1 tablespoon unsalted butter, melted

SUZETTE SAUCE
70 g (2 ½ oz) unsalted butter, at room temperature
200 g (7 oz) caster (superfine) sugar
300 ml (10 ½ fl oz) orange juice
2 oranges, zested and segmented (see glossary)
30 ml (1 fl oz) orange liqueur, such as Grand Marnier

Put the sugar and flour with a pinch of salt in the bowl of an electric mixer fitted with the whisk attachment. Whisk the milk and eggs together in a small bowl. Turn the electric mixer onto low speed and slowly add the egg mixture to the dry ingredients. Whisk until well combined, then add the melted butter.

Strain the mixture through a fine sieve into a clean bowl or container, and rest for 1 hour in the refrigerator. Heat a non-stick frying pan over medium heat and spray the pan with baking spray. Use a small ladle to pour enough batter into the pan to create a thin disc about 18 cm (7 inches) in diameter.

Cook the crepe for 1–2 minutes, until golden. Flip it over and cook for a further 1–2 minutes, until golden. The crepes will cook quickly because they are so thin.

Repeat the cooking until all the mixture is finished (8 crepes). Make sure to stack the crepes on top of each other, as this helps them to stay soft and warm.

Fold the crepes in half and then in half again to form a triangle. Reserve until needed.

To make the suzette sauce, heat the butter and sugar in a medium saucepan over medium heat for 3 minutes or until it is a light caramel colour, making sure to stir regularly, so it doesn't catch and burn.

Turn the heat off and carefully add the orange juice to deglaze. Return the saucepan to the heat and cook for 15–20 minutes, stirring, until reduced by half. Don't take it further as it will become too thick.

Remove from the heat and stir in the orange zest. Cover with plastic wrap and set aside until ready to serve.

To serve, warm the sauce in a medium saucepan and add the crepes. Tilt the pan and pour the orange liqueur over the crepes from the top side. Light it with a match or using the flame of the stove. Remove from the heat and add the orange segments and the zest. Serve in the pan or in individual dishes with cream or ice cream.

COOL TWIST
Store the crepe mixture in an airtight container with plastic wrap on the surface of the mixture for up to 3 days. Store the suzette sauce in the same way. Change the flavours and fruit: try mango with condensed milk or choc-hazelnut spread with banana (but without the alcohol).

FAIRY BREAD CAKE

Your favourite children's party food in the form of a cake. You'll have trouble deciding between a whole cake or baking it as a slice in a loaf tin. Spread with white chocolate ganache and topped with hundreds and thousands. Note that you will need to cook the cakes the day before icing them.

SERVES 18

---

450 g (1 lb) unsalted butter, at room temperature
450 g (1 lb) white chocolate (28%), chopped or buttons
450 g (1 lb/3 cups) plain (all-purpose) flour
225 g (8 oz/1½ cups) self-raising flour
600 g (1 lb 5 oz) caster (superfine) sugar
5 eggs, lightly beaten
2 teaspoons vanilla bean paste
500 g (1 lb 2 oz) hundreds and thousands (nonpareils)
16 assorted medium macarons

WHITE CHOCOLATE GANACHE
600 g (1 lb 5 oz) white chocolate (28%), chopped or buttons
300 ml (10½ fl oz) pure (pouring) cream (35% fat)
50 g (1¾ oz) unsalted butter, at room temperature

Preheat the oven to 180°C (350°F). Prepare three 18 cm (7 inch) diameter round springform cake tins by spraying the sides with cooking oil and lining the bases and sides with baking paper. Ensure the collar of the paper extends 2 cm (¾ inch) above the tin.

Put the butter and 400 ml (14 fl oz) of water into a large saucepan and stir over medium heat until the butter has melted. Remove from the heat, add the white chocolate and stir until completely melted and combined. Set aside to cool.

Combine the plain and self-raising flours, sugar and a generous pinch of salt in the bowl of an electric mixer fitted with the paddle attachment. Mix on low speed until combined, then pour in the chocolate mixture. Continue to beat while you add the eggs and vanilla paste. Beat well.

Divide the mixture between the three prepared cake tins, then smooth the top with a palette knife. Bake for 1 hour or until the cakes are golden brown and a skewer inserted in the centre of the cake comes out clean.

Cool completely in the tin, on a wire rack, then carefully remove the cakes from the tins. Wrap each cake in plastic wrap and refrigerate overnight.

To make the white chocolate ganache, put the chocolate in a heatproof bowl and set aside.

Bring the cream to the boil over medium heat and pour the hot cream over the chocolate.

Use a handheld blender to combine and create the ganache. Cover the surface with plastic food wrap and allow to cool to 40°C (105°F).

When the ganache has cooled, add the butter and use the handheld blender to mix. Pour the ganache into a clean deep tray and cover the surface with plastic wrap until ready to use. (If making the ganache at the same time as the cakes, store overnight at room temperature.)

When ready to assemble, take the 3 cakes out of the refrigerator and use a knife and ruler to trim the top flat so that each cake is 4.5 cm (1¾ inches) high. Place one of the cakes on a serving plate, using a little of the ganache to secure it in place.

Using a piping (icing) bag fitted with a size 13 plain nozzle, pipe a thick layer of the ganache onto the top of the cake and then place the second cake on top. Press the cake down gently to make sure the cake is even.

Pipe another layer of ganache onto the cake and place the final cake on top. Press down gently to make sure that the top is level and flat.

Use a palette knife to smooth out any ganache that has come out from between the layers of the cake and then apply the remaining white chocolate ganache to the outside of the cake.

Pour the hundreds and thousands into a small bowl and sprinkle over the cake, covering it completely. It may help to carefully pick the cake up.

To finish, use toothpicks to attach the macarons to the top and side of the cake. Make sure to remove the toothpicks when serving.

———————

COOL TWIST

Make the cakes ahead of time and freeze for up to 2 weeks. If you have leftover cake and ganache you can layer them in jars for a deconstructed cake treat.

———————

FAIRY BREAD SLICE

As an alternative to the round cake, try this simple alternative. You can reduce the recipe quantities by half, or make three loaf cakes in 13 x 23 x 6 cm (5 x 9¼ x 2½ inch) loaf tins. Spray the tin(s) with baking spray and line the base and sides with baking paper. Prepare the mixture as for the round cakes and bake for the same length of time.

To assemble, slice the cake into 2 cm (¾ inch) thick slices. Spread ganache on each slice, then finish with a layer of hundreds and thousands on top. Serve on a platter just like fairy bread.

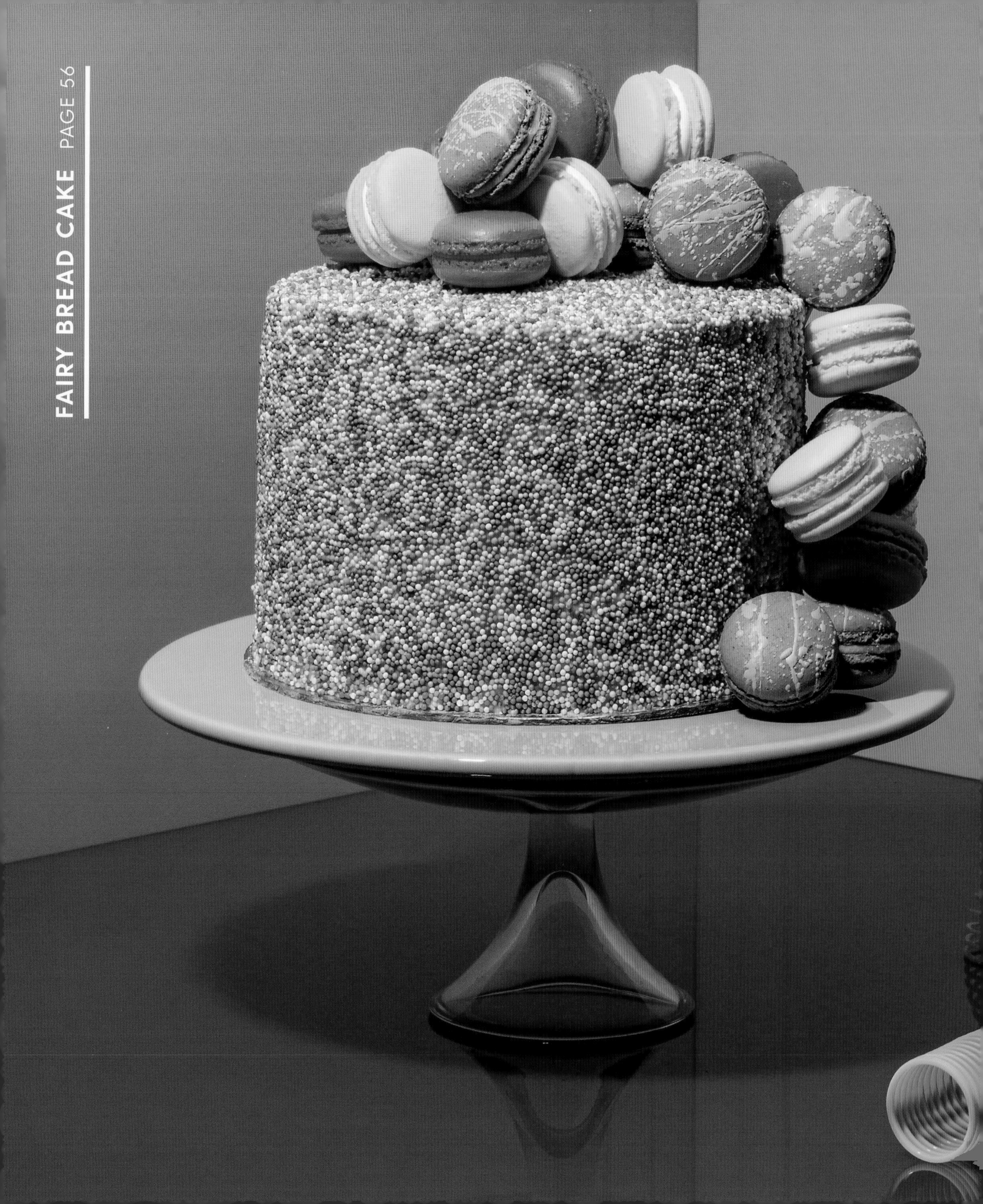

FAIRY BREAD CAKE PAGE 56

Fairy bread cake brings back the child in all of us. **Super-cool graffiti** on the macarons makes the look **really pop.**

Cannoli filled with white chocolate and dipped in caramel popcorn instead of the traditional pistachios can't go wrong. I love stacking them on top of each other into a pyramid at parties, although there's always one joker who takes one from the bottom of the stack and they all fall down.

SERVES 8

250 g (9 oz/1⅔ cups) plain (all-purpose) flour, plus extra for rolling
50 g (1¾ oz) icing (confectioners') sugar, sifted
50 g (1¾ oz) unsalted butter, at room temperature
1 egg, beaten
25 ml (1 fl oz) Marsala
1 egg white, beaten
canola oil, for frying
125 g (4½ oz) packet of caramel popcorn

WHITE CHOCOLATE CHANTILLY FILLING
120 g (4¼ oz) white chocolate, chopped or buttons
140 ml (4¾ fl oz) thickened (whipping) cream
½ vanilla bean, split and seeds scraped

To make the chantilly filling, put the chocolate in a heatproof bowl and set aside.

Combine the cream, vanilla bean and seeds in a small saucepan. Bring just to the boil over medium heat, discard the bean and pour the hot cream over the chocolate. Stir together until all the chocolate has melted.

Transfer to a container and cover the surface with plastic wrap. Stand in the refrigerator overnight.

To make the cannoli, put the flour, sugar and butter into a food processor and process until the mixture resemble fine breadcrumbs.

Add the egg and Marsala slowly, processing until it all comes together. Remove from the food processor and wrap the paste in plastic wrap. Refrigerate for 30 minutes.

Lightly flour the work surface and roll the chilled paste with a rolling pin to 2 mm (⅟₁₆ inch) thick. Cut out eight 8 cm (3¼ inch) discs.

Spray a steel cannoli tube with baking spray and wrap each disc around, then brush with egg white.

Heat the oil in a deep-fryer or large deep-sided saucepan to 180°C (350°F) or until a cube of bread dropped into the oil turns golden brown in 15 seconds. Fry the cannoli for 3–5 minutes until golden brown, transfer onto paper towel to cool.

Whisk the chantilly filling until semifirm and use a piping (icing) bag fitted with a plain nozzle to pipe the filling into the cannoli. Dip the ends of the cannoli into the caramel popcorn.

COOL TWIST
If you don't have a steel tube you can use a wooden spoon handle instead; just make sure it's sprayed well so the paste doesn't stick. You can make the cannoli up to 5 days in advance and store them in an airtight container until you are ready to fill them. Make sure the chantilly is not too firm or it will turn grainy. Try some other flavours for the filling: give them a cheesecake flavour with cream cheese filling and dip the ends in biscuit crumbs, or go traditional with ricotta cheese and crushed pistachios.

Growing up, I used to snack on fruit wraps, which were thin sheets of fruit paste on plastic paper rolled up into a tube. Now I use them for my creations.

SERVES 6

250 g (9 oz) strawberries, hulled and
   roughly chopped
25 g (1 oz) caster (superfine) sugar

Preheat the oven to 100°C (210°F).

Line a 20 x 30 cm (8 x 12 inch) baking tray with a silicone baking mat or an acetate sheet.

Put the strawberries and sugar into a blender and process until smooth.

Pour the purée onto the mat and spread evenly using a palette knife.

Bake for 1–1½ hours until the centre is set.

Immediately peel the fruit off the baking mat and lay the shiny side on freezer film. Roll firmly into a log. Cut the log into 5 cm (2 inch) wide sections. Store in an airtight container for 1–2 weeks.

COOL TWIST

It's easy to do this with other fruit such as mango and other berries. Dry it out a little more in the oven so it becomes crisp and you can use it as a garnish for a dessert.

Kids, here is your
fruit for the day!
Just fruit purée
and a little sugar
... 2 easy.

STRAWBERRIES 'N' CHAMPAGNE

When I create bubbles, it's either with a rubber ducky in a bubble bath or strawberries and Champagne: this is just how it happens. This dessert came about when I started playing around with different stabilising powders (available from specialty stores). It's a whole other side of pastry, using natural substances to stabilise items.

———

SERVES 8

———

1 kg (2 lb 4 oz) frozen whole strawberries
juice of 2 lemons
200 g (7 oz) caster (superfine) sugar
8 whole strawberries, to decorate

STRAWBERRY AND CHAMPAGNE BUBBLES
300 ml (10½ fl oz) Champagne or sparkling wine
15 g (½ oz/3 teaspoons) lecithin powder

———

Toss the strawberries, lemon juice and sugar together in a medium metal or heatproof bowl. Cover with plastic wrap and leave overnight at room temperature. This will allow the strawberries' juices to be drawn out.

Pass the macerated strawberries through a sieve, but do not press; if you allow it to pass through by itself the liquid will remain clear. Reserve the consommé until ready to make the bubbles. Store in the refrigerator if not using immediately.

To make the bubbles, mix together 600 ml (21 fl oz) of the strawberry consommé with the Champagne. Add the lecithin powder and blend with a handheld blender until the lecithin is completely dissolved.

When ready to assemble the dessert, use a handheld stick blender to create bubbles in the strawberry and Champagne mixture: do this by holding the blender sideways and slightly above the surface to introduce air and produce bubbles.

Place a strawberry on the rim of each cocktail glass then add the bubble mixture.

———

COOL TWIST

Lecithin can be purchased at health-food stores. You need a mixture to be about 1–2% of lecithin to stabilise. Consommé can be frozen and defrosted when required. Another way to make the bubbles happen is to use a water pump like the kind you would put in a fish tank.

Chocolate fondants were the biggest trend when I was in the UK just after I finished my apprenticeship. Everyone was making them and serving them with pistachio ice cream. Here I present it in a fun manner: the fondant is baked in a tin and, as you open it, you spoon over a whipped chocolate ganache for that extra kick.

SERVES 8

250 g (9 oz) dark chocolate, chopped or buttons
250 g (9 oz) unsalted butter
200 g (7 oz) caster (superfine) sugar
6 eggs
100 g (3½ oz/⅔ cup) plain (all-purpose) flour, sifted

GANACHE
250 ml (9 fl oz) pure (pouring) cream (35% fat)
130 g (4½ oz) Nestlé MILO® (chocolate malted milk powder)
130 g (4½ oz) milk chocolate, chopped or buttons

To make the ganache, bring the cream to the boil in a small saucepan over medium heat.

Put the MILO and chocolate in a stainless-steel bowl and pour the boiling cream on top. Whisk it together until the chocolate is melted and all is combined.

Transfer the ganache to the refrigerator to set for at least 1 hour, just to firm slightly.

Preheat the oven to 180°C (350°F). Prepare eight tins (see IN THE TIN) or ovenproof ramekins or mugs by greasing the inside lightly with baking spray.

Put the chocolate and butter into a microwave-proof bowl and microwave for 30 seconds at a time, stirring after each burst, until completely melted.

In an electric mixer fitted with the whisk attachment, combine the sugar and eggs on high speed for 1–2 minutes until pale and fluffy.

Reduce the speed to low and add the melted chocolate mixture. Remove from the mixer and fold in the sifted flour until well combined

Transfer the fondant mixture to a piping (icing) bag. Pipe the mixture into the prepared tins or dishes until they are three-quarters full. Transfer the tins to the refrigerator to set for 1 hour.

Bake for 20 minutes, then remove from the oven and stand for 5 minutes.

Serve in the tin or dish with the ganache on the side ready to spoon over.

IN THE TIN
To bake in tins, you'll need eight small tins, the kind with the pop-off top. The tins should measure 7 cm (2¾ inch) diameter x 8 cm (3¼ inches) deep. You can open them from the base to remove the contents and keep the pop-top intact. Make sure they are really clean and dry before using them. Keep the base and tape it back on with masking tape before baking.

COOL TWIST
You can store the mixture in the fridge for up to 4 days before baking. If you're using ramekins or heatproof mugs, you might need to make a test batch to check the cooking times. Overcooking them means losing the runny self-saucing centre; undercook them and the whole thing turns to mush.

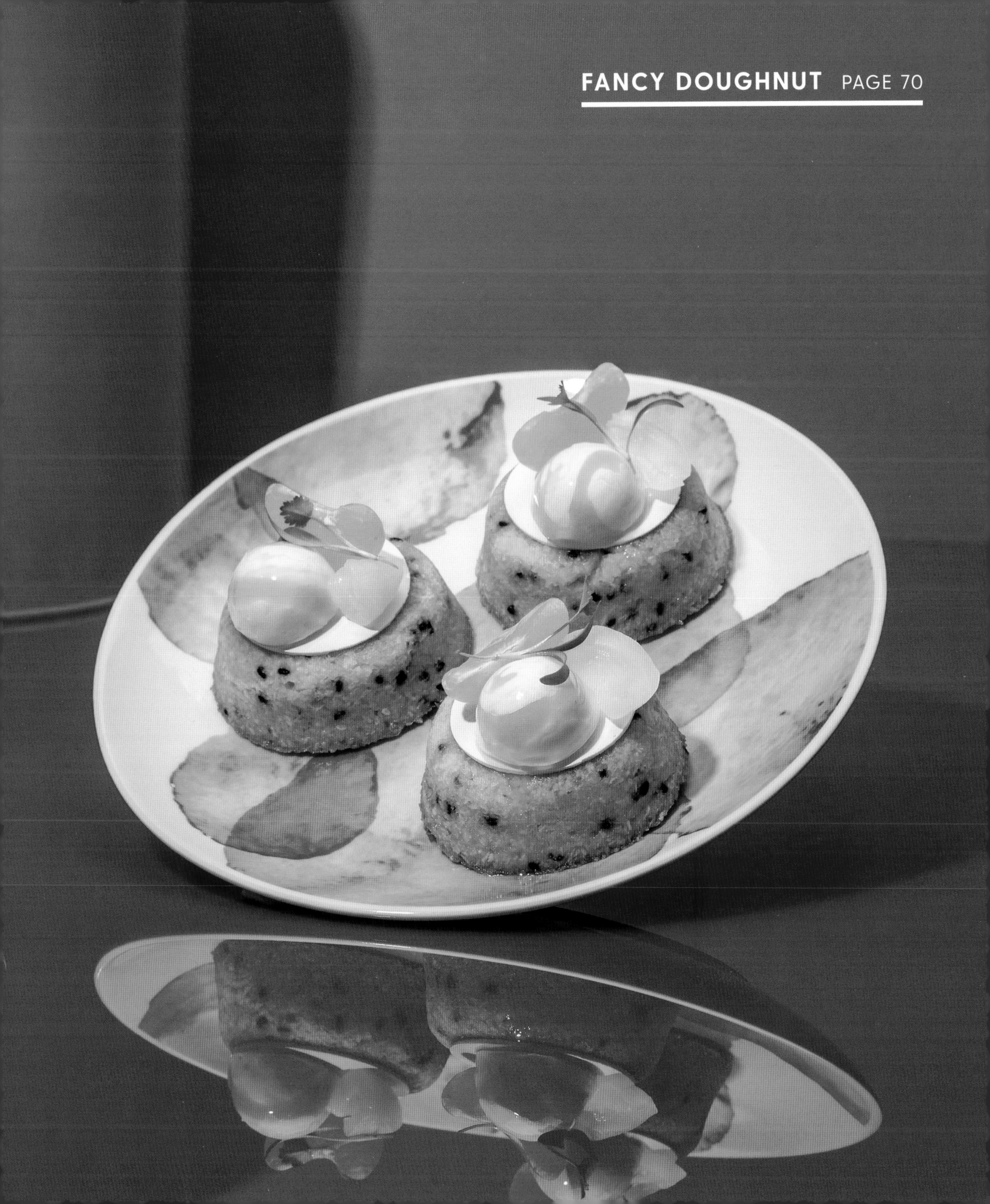

FANCY DOUGHNUT PAGE 70

A classic orange and poppyseed cake gets a modern twist to make a gluten-free dessert more exciting.

MAKES 12

CITRUS AND SESAME CAKE
2 mandarins (clementines)
2 oranges
4 eggs
320 g (11¼ oz) caster (superfine) sugar
2 teaspoons baking powder, sifted
200 g (7 oz/2 cups) almond meal, sifted
200 g (7 oz) desiccated coconut
3 teaspoons black sesame seeds
3 teaspoons white sesame seeds

Put the mandarins and oranges in a medium saucepan and cover with cold water. Bring to the boil, then reduce the heat and simmer for 1 hour, topping up with more water to ensure the fruit is fully submerged. The fruit should be very soft. Remove the fruit from the water and set it aside to cool.

When cool enough to handle, roughly chop the fruit and put it into a food processor. Blend until smooth.

Preheat the oven to 160°C (315°F). Lightly grease 12 round doughnut moulds.

In the bowl of an electric mixer fitted with the whisk attachment, combine the eggs and the caster sugar. Whisk on high speed until light and fluffy. Reduce the speed and gradually add the baking powder, almond meal and coconut. When well combined, remove from the electric mixer.

Use a spatula to fold in the sesame seeds along with the puréed mandarins and oranges until everything is completely combined.

Use a piping (icing) bag or a spoon to fill each doughnut mould three-quarters full. Bake for 15–20 minutes or until a skewer inserted into the thickest part of a doughnut comes out clean.

Set aside to cool in the moulds then carefully remove the doughnuts from the moulds and reserve until needed for assembly. The doughnuts can be frozen in an airtight container for up to 4 weeks.

PASSIONFRUIT AND LEMON CURD
60 ml (2 fl oz/¼ cup) lemon juice
60 ml (2 fl oz/¼ cup) passionfruit juice
3 eggs
1 egg yolk
130 g (4½ oz) caster (superfine) sugar
50 g (1¾ oz) unsalted butter, at room temperature

Combine the lemon and passionfruit juices in a medium saucepan and bring them to the boil over medium heat.

Meanwhile, in a small bowl, whisk together the eggs, egg yolk and caster sugar.

Pour the boiling juices into the egg mixture and whisk until combined. Return to the saucepan and whisk constantly over medium heat until the mixture starts to thicken and coats the back of a spoon. Remove from the heat and strain through a fine sieve.

Allow the curd to cool down to about body temperature, then use a handheld blender to mix in the butter, blending for 2–3 minutes until the curd is smooth and silky.

Transfer the curd to a clean container and cover the surface with plastic wrap, so that a skin does not form on top of the curd. Reserve in the refrigerator for up to 5 days until needed for assembly.

MANGO JELLY

125 ml (4 fl oz/½ cup) mango purée (see glossary)
2 teaspoons caster (superfine) sugar
½ sheet titanium-strength gelatine, softened in
    cold water

You will need twelve 3 cm (1¼ inch) sphere moulds.
Put the moulds in the freezer before adding the jelly.
This will prevent the jelly from running.

Combine the mango and caster sugar in a small
saucepan. Bring to a simmer, stirring until the sugar
has dissolved, then remove from the heat.

Gently squeeze excess liquid from the gelatine
and add it to the warm purée, stirring until the
gelatine is completely dissolved. Strain the liquid
and set aside to cool to room temperature.

Use a clean finger to make a swirl of the mango
jelly mixture on the inside of each of the chilled
sphere moulds. Return the moulds to the freezer to
set completely before adding the yoghurt mousse.

YOGHURT MOUSSE

1 tablespoon caster (superfine) sugar
1 tablespoon lime juice
2 sheets titanium-strength gelatine, softened in
    cold water
125 g (4½ oz) plain yoghurt
125 ml (4 fl oz/½ cup) pure (pouring) cream,
    lightly whipped

Bring the sugar and lime juice to the boil in a small
saucepan over medium heat. Remove from the heat.
Squeeze excess liquid from the gelatine and add it
to the sugar syrup. Strain the mixture into a bowl
and set aside to cool.

Gradually add the cooled lime mixture to the
yoghurt, whisking constantly. Fold through the lightly
whipped cream. Pour the mixture into the frozen
sphere moulds and return the moulds to the freezer
to set completely.

TO ASSEMBLE

300 g (10½ oz) white chocolate (28%), tempered
    (see page 232)
1 tablespoon BRUSH ME PRETTY nappage
    (see page 232)
1 mandarin (clementine), peeled, pith and seeds
    removed and segmented
8 lychees, peeled and halved
1 small handful of baby coriander (cilantro) leaves

Line a flat tray with a sheet of acetate, then use a
palette knife to spread a thin layer of the tempered
white chocolate.

When the chocolate has just set, use a 5 cm
(2 inch) diameter round cutter to cut out 12 circles.

When the chocolate has completely set, place
a piece of baking paper and then a second flat tray
on top. Transfer to the refrigerator for 10 minutes to
set. Remove the trays from the refrigerator and flip
them over, so that the shiny side of the chocolate is
on top. Remove the top tray and the acetate sheet.
Leave the discs on the baking paper until needed.

Put the passionfruit and lemon curd into a piping
(icing) bag and fill the centre of each doughnut with
the passionfruit and lemon curd, until level with the
top of the doughnut. Centre a white chocolate disc
on top of each doughnut.

Warm the nappage. Carefully unmould the
frozen yoghurt domes and dip each one into the
nappage, allowing any excess nappage to drain off.
Place a dome onto each of the doughnuts, to the
left-hand side.

Top each doughnut with a mandarin segment,
half a lychee and a coriander sprig.

COOL TWIST

I've made this recipe using ants — yes, ants — by
replacing the sesame seeds with edible ants. (I have
a friend who farms edible bugs.) Ants have a citrus
taste, so it worked really well and tasted good!

Sherbet fizz is a simple recipe that I often serve in a test tube for guests to pour onto desserts, or in a long straw, which is a play on childhood memories.

SERVES 20

1 teaspoon citric acid
1 teaspoon bicarbonate of soda (baking soda)
1 teaspoon tartaric acid
110 g (3¾ oz) icing (confectioners') sugar
½ teaspoon green food-colouring powder

LIME POWDER
50 g (1¾ oz) caster (superfine) sugar
zest of 3 limes

To make the lime powder, preheat the oven or a dehydrator to 100°C (210°F). Combine the sugar with 60 ml (2 fl oz/¼ cup) of water in a small saucepan over medium heat. Bring to the boil. Remove from the heat and add the lime zest. Return to low heat and simmer for 5 minutes.

Pass through a fine sieve and discard the sugar syrup, reserving the zest. Pat dry with paper towel.

Spread the zest on a baking tray lined with baking paper and dry in the oven or a dehydrator for 1 hour or until crisp.

Cool on the tray, then use a coffee grinder to grind until very fine. Store the lime powder in an airtight container until ready to use.

In a medium bowl, mix together all of the ingredients and 3 teaspoons of the lime powder. Sift through a fine dry sieve.

Take a colourful plastic drinking straw, flatten one end and melt it together with a small flame (use a stove lighter) so it forms a seal. Use a small funnel or folded baking paper to fill the straw three-quarters full with the sherbet and then seal the open end of the straw using a pair of heated metal tongs to squeeze it together.

COOL TWIST
Make sure the sherbet is stored in a dry place. You can swap the lime for any other citrus fruit if you prefer.

Sherbet fizz **reminds me of the old days** when **milk bars were still around,** and a bag of **1 cent mixed lollies** were every kid's idea of **heaven.**

CLOUDS

I used to do crepe soufflés when I was an apprentice, with a crepe on the outside and soufflé mixture inside. It's basically a two-in-one dessert that's got the 'wow' factor when it comes out of the oven. These mini versions of a crepe soufflé are great for entertaining at home if you want to show off and impress your guests.

————

SERVES 8

————

8 CREPES, 18 cm (7 inch) diameter (see page 53)

SOUFFLE FILLING
250 ml (9 fl oz/1 cup) milk
½ vanilla bean, split and seeds scraped
120 g (4¼ oz) caster (superfine) sugar
3 eggs, separated
40 g (1½ oz) custard powder
zest and juice of 1 orange
2 teaspoons orange liqueur, such as Grand Marnier

————

Prepare 8 crepes following the recipe and instructions on page 53.

To make the soufflé filling, combine the milk and vanilla bean with the seeds in a medium saucepan over medium heat. Bring to the boil.

In a small bowl combine 100 g (3½ oz) of the sugar and the egg yolks and whisk until completely combined. Add the custard powder and whisk together until all is combined and there are no lumps.

Discard the vanilla bean and pour half of the hot milk over the custard mixture. Whisk until combined. Return the saucepan of milk to medium heat and bring back to the boil.

Once the milk has come to the boil, pour the egg mixture into it. Continue cooking over medium heat for about 5 minutes, stirring regularly so it doesn't catch, until it thickens and starts bubbling.

Pour the custard into a deep tray and cover the surface with plastic wrap. Transfer to the refrigerator to cool.

Preheat the oven to 220°C (425°F). Line a baking tray with baking paper and take the custard out of the refrigerator to come to room temperature.

In an electric mixer fitted with the whisk attachment, whisk the egg whites on high speed until they form soft peaks. Add the remaining sugar and continue beating to stiff peaks.

Transfer the custard to a medium bowl and whisk by hand to soften, adding the orange zest and the liqueur.

Fold in the egg white, making sure not to overwork it, which affects the stability.

Cut the crepes to 8 cm (3¼ inch) discs with a cutter. Place 1 teaspoon of soufflé filling in the centre of each crepe and fold the crepe in half over the filling. They will look like fluffy clouds.

Put the crepes on the prepared baking tray and bake for 10–12 minutes. Serve straight from the oven before the clouds deflate.

————

COOL TWIST

Flavour the soufflé mixture by adding fruit or a sauce, to add a little excitement when cutting it. Leave out the alcohol if you prefer. Dust with icing sugar so the soufflés look like mini clouds. You can also make the soufflé in a ramekin without the crepe.

Burgers are so fun and fashionable that I decided to turn a choux bun into a burger and place it in a mini burger box. It's always nice to create something with a fun twist. I served my first batch of choux burgers at Sweet Street in 2017 and they went viral on social media and with everyone's tastebuds too.

SERVES 5

VANILLA SABLE

75 g (2¾ oz) unsalted butter, at room temperature
50 g (1¾ oz) caster (superfine) sugar
½ vanilla bean, seeds scraped
100 g (3½ oz/⅔ cups) plain (all-purpose) flour

In an electric mixer fitted with the paddle attachment, beat together the butter, sugar and the vanilla seeds on medium speed until well combined.

Use a rolling pin to roll the sable out between two sheets of baking paper until it is 3–4 mm (⅛ inch) thick.

Transfer the sable to a flat tray and put it in the freezer for 30 minutes or until firm.

Use a 6 cm (2½ inch) diameter cutter to cut out five discs and lay them on a baking tray lined with baking paper. Set the discs aside in the refrigerator until the choux is ready to bake.

PÂTE À CHOUX

80 ml (2½ fl oz/⅓ cup) milk
60 g (2¼ oz) unsalted butter, at room temperature
1 teaspoon caster (superfine) sugar
1 teaspoon salt
80 g (2¾ oz) plain (all-purpose) flour
2 eggs, lightly beaten

Preheat the oven to 190°C (375°F).

Put 80 ml (2½ fl oz/⅓ cup) of water in a medium saucepan with the milk, butter, caster sugar and salt. Bring it to the boil over medium heat.

Add the flour and stir constantly until the mixture thickens and pulls away from the side of the pan. Cook for a further 30–60 seconds to develop the gluten.

Transfer the mix to the bowl of an electric mixer fitted with the paddle attachment and beat on a medium speed until 60 per cent of the heat has dispersed.

Add the eggs, a little at a time, until you achieve a glossy paste that should just fall off the beater.

Transfer the paste to a piping (icing) bag fitted with a size 11 plain nozzle. Spray a heavy baking sheet with baking spray and then pipe the paste in five 7 cm (2¾ inch) rounds. Place a disc of sable on top of each round.

Bake for 30–40 minutes until puffed and golden. Remove from the oven and pass a metal spatula underneath each choux bun to release it from the tray. The choux pastry should feel hollow when lifted off the tray. Set aside to cool.

PEANUT BUTTER CREMEUX

60 ml (2 fl oz/¼ cup) milk
60 ml (2 fl oz/¼ cup) pure (pouring) cream (35% fat)
50 g (1¾ oz) white chocolate, chopped or buttons
40 g (1½ oz) crunchy peanut butter
30 g (1 oz) caster (superfine) sugar
2 egg yolks
2 sheets titanium-strength gelatine, soaked in cold water to soften

Put the milk and cream in a small saucepan over medium heat and bring just to the boil.

Meanwhile, put the white chocolate and peanut butter in a medium bowl and set aside. Whisk the caster sugar and egg yolks in a separate medium bowl until well combined

Once the cream mixture has just come to the boil, remove it from the heat and pour half into the egg mixture. Whisk well to combine. Pour the egg mixture back into the remaining cream mixture in the saucepan and return to medium heat. Continue to cook, stirring constantly until the mixture reaches 65°C (use a thermometer) or coats the back of a spoon. Remove from the heat.

Squeeze out the gelatine to remove excess water and add it to the anglaise, stirring well until the gelatine has dissolved completely. Strain through a fine sieve over the chocolate and peanut butter and whisk until completely combined. Transfer to a pouring jug.

Lay a silicone mat with 6 cm (2½ inch) disc moulds on a flat baking tray and pour 50 ml (1¾ fl oz) of the cremeux into each mould.

Carefully transfer the tray to the freezer and allow to completely freeze.

RASPBERRY JELLY
40 g (1½ oz) caster (superfine) sugar
185 ml (6 fl oz/¾ cup) raspberry purée (see glossary)
4 sheets titanium-strength gelatine, soaked in cold water to soften

Put the sugar into a small saucepan with 200 ml (7 fl oz) of water and bring it to the boil; meanwhile, put the raspberry purée into a medium bowl.

When the sugar syrup has come to the boil, remove from the heat and whisk in the gelatine. Strain and allow to cool.

Line a 20 x 30 x 1 cm (8 x 12 x ⅜ inch) tray with plastic wrap or an acetate sheet. Lay the tray flat in the freezer and carefully pour the jelly mixture into the tray. Freeze for 1 hour or until set.

Remove the jelly from the tray and cut into five 7 cm (2¾ inch) squares. Keep the jelly in the freezer until you are ready to assemble the burger

----

WHITE CHOCOLATE CHANTILLY CREAM
600 ml (21 fl oz) thickened (whipping) cream
1 vanilla bean, split and seeds scraped
300 g (10½ oz) white chocolate (28%), chopped or buttons
6 sheets titanium-strength gelatine, soaked in cold water to soften

Put the cream, vanilla bean and seeds in a small saucepan and bring just to the boil over medium heat.

Meanwhile, put the white chocolate into a medium heatproof bowl. When the cream has just come to the boil, remove it from the heat and discard the vanilla bean. Stir in the softened gelatine and pour the mixture over the chocolate. Stir until all the chocolate has melted.

Transfer to a container and cover the surface with plastic wrap. Keep in the refrigerator overnight.

TO ASSEMBLE
50 g (1¾ oz) caramel popcorn

Carefully cut the choux buns in half horizontally.

Remove the peanut butter cremeux from the moulds and place one on the bottom half of each choux bun.

Put the white chocolate chantilly cream in the bowl of an electric mixer fitted with the whisk attachment and whisk to semi-firm peaks. Fill a piping (icing) bag fitted with a size 15 plain nozzle with the whisked chantilly. Pipe around the edge of the peanut butter cremeux.

In the centre of the cremeux, place 10 g (⅜ oz) of caramel popcorn in each burger.

Remove the jelly squares from the freezer and discard any plastic. Place a jelly square on top of the popcorn and then finish the burger off with the top half of the bun.

COOL TWIST
Colour some chocolate yellow to make a slice of 'cheese' for the burger. Make the choux in a long oval to look like a baguette. I use the same choux mix to make savoury eclairs and fill them with a mixture of chicken, celery and micro herbs. It's cute and super-tasty.

How can a cold-set milk dessert be so simple, yet still be everyone's favourite? Set it in individual moulds and plate it with fruit and biscotti; serve it in a glass bowl as a layered trifle; or pipe the mixture into shot glasses and top with berries and mini meringues for crunch. So similar, so easy ... yet so different.

3SOME PANNA COTTA

This tropical take on panna cotta is served in a glass bowl like a trifle so you're able to see the layers.

SERVES 8

VANILLA PANNA COTTA
50 ml (1¾ fl oz) milk
1 tablespoon caster (superfine) sugar
1 vanilla bean, split and seeds scraped
1 sheet titanium-strength gelatine, soaked in
    cold water to soften
150 ml (5½ fl oz) pure (pouring) cream (35% fat)

COCONUT TAPIOCA
50 g (1¾ oz) tapioca
175 ml (6 fl oz) milk
250 ml (9 fl oz/1 cup) coconut cream
75 g (2¾ oz/⅓ cup) caster (superfine) sugar

MANGO AND PASSIONFRUIT JELLY (gelatine)
50 ml (1¾ fl oz) passionfruit purée (see glossary)
140 ml (4¾ fl oz) mango purée (see glossary)
1 tablespoon caster (superfine) sugar
1 sheet titanium-strength gelatine, soaked in cold
    water to soften

TO ASSEMBLE
½ pineapple, peeled, halved and thinly sliced
1 mango, peeled and cheeks cut into thin slices
2 passionfruit
1 small handful baby coriander (cilantro), to garnish

In a small saucepan, combine the milk, sugar and the vanilla bean and seeds and bring to the boil over medium heat.

Remove from the heat and stir in the softened gelatine until completely dissolved. Pass through a fine sieve over the cream and stir together.

Transfer the mixture to the refrigerator and leave to partially set, which ensures that the vanilla seeds are evenly dispersed throughout the mix.

Line a flat tray with plastic wrap and set a large glass serving bowl on it. When the panna cotta has partially set, pour it into the bowl, making sure the surface is level. Transfer to the refrigerator for 1 hour or until set.

To make the coconut tapioca, fill a medium saucepan with water and bring it to the boil over high heat. Reduce the heat to low and stir in the tapioca.

Simmer the tapioca for 15–20 minutes until clear, stirring occasionally so that the tapioca does not stick to the bottom of the pot. Remove from the heat and strain, discarding the water. Rinse with cold water until the tapioca cools completely.

Gently stir the tapioca so that it does not stick together, then transfer to a medium bowl and set aside until needed.

In a small saucepan, bring the milk, coconut cream and sugar just to the boil. Remove from the heat, pour onto the tapioca and stir until well combined. Cover with plastic wrap and refrigerate until needed.

To make the jelly, bring the two fruit purées and the sugar just to the boil in a small saucepan over high heat. Remove from the heat and stir in the softened gelatine until dissolved.

Strain the jelly mixture into a plastic container and cover the surface with plastic wrap or freezer film. Set aside to cool.

When the jelly mixture is cool but not yet set, gently pour a thin layer on top of the set panna cotta in the glass bowl. Return to the refrigerator for the jelly to set.

To assemble, take the panna cotta and jelly out of the refrigerator, and spoon the coconut tapioca evenly over the jelly.

Arrange the elements of the tropical compote on top. Then decorate with the baby coriander.

3SOME TWIST
Make sure that the panna cotta is partially set before you pour it into the bowl, otherwise the vanilla seeds fall to the bottom. The panna cotta must be set and the jelly cooled before pouring the jelly on top of the panna cotta, or the panna cotta will come to the top.

Twenty desserts to choose from on a menu and the panna cotta always goes first: it's a star.

SERVES 8

3 quantities of partially set VANILLA PANNA COTTA mixture (see page 83)

BISCOTTI
4 egg whites
130 g (4½ oz) caster (superfine) sugar
175 g (6 oz) plain (all-purpose) flour
80 g (2¾ oz/¾ cup) hazelnuts
80 g (2¾ oz/½ cup) almonds
80 g (2¾ oz) pistachios

STRAWBERRY CONSOMME
250 g (9 oz) frozen strawberries, coarsely chopped
50 g (1¾ oz) caster (superfine) sugar
juice of ½ lemon

BERRY GARNISH
250 g (9 oz) strawberries, hulled and halved
150 g (5½ oz) raspberries
1 handful baby basil

To make the strawberry consommé, toss together the frozen strawberries, sugar and lemon juice in a metal or heatproof bowl. Cover the bowl with plastic wrap and set aside on the kitchen bench overnight to draw out the strawberry juice.

Pass the strawberry mixture through a sieve. Do not press the strawberry pulp through; allow it to pass through by itself so that the liquid remains clear. Discard the pulp and reserve the liquid in the refrigerator until needed.

Line a flat tray with plastic wrap and set eight dariole moulds on it. Lightly spray with baking spray. Pour 80 ml (2½ fl oz/⅓ cup) of the partially set panna cotta mixture into each mould. Put the tray in the refrigerator for 1 hour or until set.

Meanwhile, make the biscotti. Preheat the oven to 160°C (315°F) and line a baking tray with baking paper. Using an electric mixer fitted with the whisk attachment, whisk the egg whites in a clean dry bowl until soft peaks form. Reduce the speed and gradually add the caster sugar, whisking well after each addition.

Return to high speed and whisk the mixture for 3–4 minutes until firm peaks have formed. Take the bowl off the mixer and fold in the plain flour, followed by the nuts. Make sure not to overmix or the meringue will break down.

Transfer the mixture to the prepared tray and form into a 45 cm x 5 cm (18 inch x 2 inch) log. Smooth the surface with a little water, but make sure not to use too much or it will make the biscotti spread.

Bake for 30–35 minutes until lightly golden brown. Allow to cool and then cut into 5 mm (¼ inch) slices.

Reduce the heat of the oven to 100°C (210°F) and lay a fresh sheet of baking paper on the tray. Lay the slices of biscotti on the tray and cook for 15–20 minutes until crisp and pale golden.

To assemble the dessert, carefully turn the panna cotta out onto serving plates.

Arrange the strawberries and raspberries around the panna cotta and then finish with two biscotti and garnish with baby basil. When ready to serve, pour the strawberry consommé around the panna cotta.

3SOME TWIST
Make sure to spray the panna cotta moulds with baking spray so the panna cotta will not stick to the mould. If you're having trouble getting them out of the mould, try sitting the mould in warm water, although this will start to melt the outside of the panna cotta.

This recipe is about using up leftovers. I put it in shot glasses to make sweet canapés or small portions for a buffet. It's a dish that's tasty, looks great and, better yet, it's easy to make.

10 SHOTS

1 quantity of partially set VANILLA PANNA COTTA mixture (see page 83)

STRAWBERRY JELLY
1 sheet titanium-strength gelatine, soaked in cold water to soften
120 ml (4 fl oz) STRAWBERRY CONSOMME (see page 84)

MERINGUE KISSES
3½ egg whites
100 g (3½ oz) caster (superfine) sugar
50 g (1¾ oz) icing (confectioners') sugar, sifted

BERRY TOPPING
125 g (4½ oz) strawberries, hulled and quartered
75 g (2¾ oz) raspberries, halved

Line a flat tray with plastic wrap and place the 10 shot glasses on the tray. Put 1 tablespoon of the partially set panna cotta mixture into each glass. Transfer to the refrigerator for 1 hour or until set.

Meanwhile, make the jelly. In a small saucepan, bring 60 ml (2 fl oz/¼ cup) of water just to the boil over high heat. Remove from the heat and stir in the softened gelatine until dissolved completely.

Strain the gelatine mixture over 120 ml (4 fl oz) of the strawberry essence. Stir to combine and allow to cool to 20°C (68°F) or a cool room temperature.

Carefully add 2 teaspoons of the strawberry jelly to each shot glass on top of the set panna cotta. Return to the refrigerator for the jelly to set.

To make the meringue kisses, preheat the oven or a dehydrator to 74°C (165°F). Line a baking tray with baking paper and set aside.

In a clean dry bowl of an electric mixer fitted with the whisk attachment, whisk the egg whites on high speed until soft peaks form. Reduce the speed and gradually add the caster sugar.

Return to high speed and whisk for about 5 minutes until the meringue is thick and glossy and sugar has dissolved. Rub a little meringue between your fingers. If it still feels 'gritty', continue to whisk until the sugar has dissolved. Firm peaks need to be achieved.

Remove from the mixer and fold in the icing sugar. Be quick or the meringue will become runny.

Using a piping (icing) bag fitted with a size 9 plain nozzle, pipe dollops of the meringue onto the prepared tray and bake for 2½ hours or until dried out. Keep checking to make sure the temperature isn't too high, as you don't want the meringue to colour. Set aside to cool, then store in an airtight container until required.

Toss the berries together and spoon them into the top of the shot glasses. Finish off with meringue kisses.

3SOME TWIST
You can store the panna cotta and jelly in the fridge for up to 5 days. To switch things up, feel free to change the flavour of the jelly, the fruit in the topping or even the garnish.

My mother is a whiz in the kitchen, but there's no such thing as measuring: it's all about the sight, taste and feel that makes a kick-arse cook. Being Greek Cypriot has been a massive bonus as I get older; but when I was young and craved the steak-and-three-veg my friends ate, there was only haloumi and spanakopita for me.

KOURABIEDES

Kourabiedes are a traditional Easter and Christmas biscuit, made with almonds, butter and icing sugar. They say the icing sugar represents the snow and the alcohol that Santa would drink, or so I was told back when I was younger.

MAKES 30

---

500 g (1 lb 2 oz) unsalted butter, at room temperature
250 g (9 oz) caster (superfine) sugar
2 eggs, beaten
1 vanilla bean, seeds scraped
1 tablespoon brandy or whisky
1 kg (2 lb 4 oz) self-raising flour
250 g (9 oz) blanched almonds, roasted and processed to coarse crumbs
2 teaspoons baking powder
1 kg (2 lb 4 oz) icing (confectioners') sugar

Preheat the oven to 160°C (315°F). Line a baking tray with baking paper.

Combine the butter and caster sugar in the bowl of an electric mixer fitted with the paddle attachment. Beat for 3 minutes or until light and fluffy.

Reduce the speed and gradually add the eggs, then the vanilla seeds and brandy or whisky.

Remove from the mixer and fold through the dry ingredients, to make a thick paste.

Shape 25 g (1 oz) or a full tablespoon of the mixture into an oval between the palms of your hands. Pinch a ridge along the top of each biscuit and place them on the prepared tray, leaving space between each one.

Bake for 20–25 minutes, until golden, then cool on the tray for at least 1–2 hours.

Store the cold biscuits in an airtight container, covered with the icing sugar. When ready to serve, lift the biscuits out of the icing sugar and shake off any excess.

MUM'S TWIST

If the biscuits are still warm when you put them into the icing sugar, it turns the icing sugar yellow and it dissolves too. Kourabiedes will keep for 2–3 weeks in an airtight container.

Every Greek household would give these to other families **as presents at Christmas time.** The icing sugar all around the lips **made it extra tasty and messy too.**

This is my favourite Greek dessert: one of those things that taste better straight out of the oven with syrup poured over. My mother would always tell me off for attacking the tray before it had cooled down. This recipe is completely Mum's: I haven't adjusted it nor have I added my French training. This is what I grew up with and I want you to experience a little part of me too. You'll come across loads of different recipes for this dish, but in my eyes this is the perfect way — Mum's way.

SERVES 20

600 ml (21 fl oz) milk
2 tablespoons vanilla sugar (from the supermarket)
2 eggs
70 g (2½ oz) caster (superfine) sugar
125 g (4½ oz) fine semolina
25 g (1 oz) unsalted butter
finely grated zest of 1 lemon
375 g (13 oz) packet frozen filo pastry
    (about 20 sheets)
400 g (14 oz) unsalted butter, melted

SYRUP
1 kg (2 lb 4 oz) caster (superfine) sugar
1 cinnamon stick
10 whole cloves
juice of 1 lemon

Combine all of the syrup ingredients in a medium saucepan with 750 ml (26 fl oz/3 cups) of cold water and bring to the boil. Stir until the sugar has dissolved.

Refrigerate the syrup until completely cool. The syrup is best made the day before so that it is really cold when you pour it onto the hot galaktoboureko.

Put the milk into a medium saucepan with the vanilla sugar and bring to the boil.

Meanwhile, whisk together the eggs and caster sugar until pale in colour and well combined. Add the semolina to the egg mixture and continue whisking until well combined.

When the milk has come to the boil, add the semolina mixture. Whisk for a further 5 minutes over medium heat until the mixture has thickened.

Remove from the heat and stir in the butter and lemon zest. Set aside at room temperature until needed.

Preheat the oven to 165°C (320°F). Lay the filo sheets on a clean work surface, cover with a clean tea towel (dish towel) that has been slightly dampened with cold water. This is so the thin sheets of filo don't dry out.

Lightly brush a deep-sided 20 x 30 x 4 cm (8 x 12 x 1½ inch) baking tray with melted butter.

Lay 1 sheet of filo in the base of the baking tray and brush with a little melted butter. Top with another filo sheet and lightly brush with melted butter. Repeat with another 8 filo sheets and melted butter. Make sure that the filo sheets overhang the sides of the dish so it holds in the semolina custard.

Pour the semolina custard into the baking dish. Repeat the layering with the remaining filo sheets and the remaining melted butter.

Use a small sharp knife to score the top of the galaktoboureko into 20 rectangles. Brush with the remaining melted butter and sprinkle a little water over the top. Bake for 60 minutes or until golden.

While the dish is still hot, pour the cold syrup over it.

MUM'S TWIST
Make sure to cut the filo layers to shape before baking, but don't cut right to the bottom: if it hasn't been done before baking you won't be able to do it after. When cooking the semolina custard, make sure you keep whisking so that it doesn't catch on the bottom of the saucepan.

GALAKTOBOUREKO MESA-STO-SINI (in a tray)

Yoyos, known to Greeks as **kok** (the reason for the **nickname** is obvious), are always one of the **bestselling sweets** at any Greek pastry shop.

YOYOS (kok)

As a child I would buy yoyos from a pastry shop and sit and eat them with my godmother Angela, my second mum.

MAKES 25–30

6 eggs, separated
140 g (5 oz) caster (superfine) sugar
125 g (4½ oz) plain (all-purpose) flour, sifted
50 g (1¾ oz) cornflour (cornstarch), sifted
300 g (10½ oz) dark chocolate (53%), chopped or buttons

VANILLA SYRUP

200 g (7 oz) caster (superfine) sugar
1 vanilla bean, split and seeds scraped
1 tablespoon lemon juice

VANILLA CUSTARD FILLING

1 litre (35 fl oz/4 cups) milk
100 g (3½ oz) unsalted butter
1 vanilla bean, split and seeds scraped
12 egg yolks
200 g (7 oz) caster (superfine) sugar
100 g (3½ oz) custard powder

To make the syrup, combine all of the ingredients with 200 ml (7 fl oz) of water in a small saucepan and stir. Bring to the boil over medium heat. Remove from the heat and set aside to cool completely before using.

To make the custard filling, combine the milk, butter and the vanilla bean and seeds in a small saucepan over medium heat and bring the mixture to the boil. Meanwhile, whisk together the egg yolks, sugar and custard powder. Pour half the boiling milk mixture into the egg mixture and stir well. Return the mixture to the pan with the remaining milk mixture.

Return to medium heat, whisking until the custard becomes quite thick. Make sure it does not catch on the bottom of the saucepan.

Pour the custard into a heatproof bowl and discard the vanilla bean. Cover the surface with plastic wrap and transfer to the refrigerator to cool completely before using.

Preheat the oven to 200°C (400°F). Line one large or two small baking trays with baking paper.

In an electric mixer fitted with the whisk attachment, whisk the egg yolks with 90 g (3¼ oz) of the caster sugar on high speed until pale and thick. Transfer to a bowl.

Using a clean dry bowl and whisk attachment, whisk the egg whites starting on low speed and gradually increasing to high speed, to soft peaks.

Reduce the speed to low and slowly add the remaining sugar, then increase the speed to high and whisk to firm peaks.

Fold half of the egg white mixture into the yolk mixture. The fold through the flour and cornflour. Fold in the remaining egg white mixture; make sure not to over mix the sponge.

Put the mixture into a piping (icing) bag fitted with a plain size 13 nozzle. Pipe 5 cm (2 inch) discs onto the prepared trays, making sure there is plenty of space between each one. Bake in the oven for 10–12 minutes until golden. Allow to cool on the tray. The mixture should make 50–60 sponge discs.

To assemble, match the sponge cookies up into pairs. Turn one of each pair over so that the flat side faces up. Brush the flat side with the sugar syrup.

Take the custard filling out of the refrigerator and beat with a spatula until smooth. Fill a piping (icing) bag fitted with a plain size 15 nozzle with the custard filling and pipe it on to the cookie just inside the edge.

Turn the other discs over and brush the flat side with the sugar syrup. Place the matching cookie on top of the custard so that the flat side coated with sugar syrup is touching the custard. Gently squeeze together, so that the custard cream reaches the edge of the cookie.

Put the chocolate into a microwave-proof bowl and melt in 40-second bursts, stirring between each burst, until two-thirds of the chocolate is melted. Stir the chocolate until it's completely melted and then temper down to 30°C (86°F) – see page 232.

Dip the top of a Kok into the chocolate and allow the excess chocolate to run off. Place the Kok back onto the tray with the chocolate side up and allow to set completely.

Repeat for the remaining Kok. Fill a paper piping (icing) bag with the remaining chocolate and pipe a spiral on top of each Kok.

We would always eat loukoumades at Greek festivals, where there would be giagiás ('ya-yas') making them. The old ladies would be like machines squeezing them between their hands and just popping out perfect round balls that would fry light and crispy and soak up all the sugar syrup and chopped walnuts. This recipe is my version: I still dunk them into honey syrup, but I add caramel popcorn and choc-hazelnut dipping sauce.

SERVES 6

250 ml (9 fl oz/1 cup) warm water
5 g (⅛ oz) fresh yeast
250 g (9 oz/1⅔ cups) plain (all-purpose) flour
1 tablespoon caster (superfine) sugar
1 teaspoon vanilla paste
canola oil, for deep-frying and for oiling your hands
caramel popcorn, to serve

HONEY SYRUP
110 g (3¾ oz/½ cup) caster (superfine) sugar
200 ml (7 fl oz) honey
1 cinnamon stick
5 whole cloves
1 vanilla bean, seeds scraped
juice of 1 lemon

CHOCOLATE DIPPING SAUCE
80 g (2¾ oz) choc-hazelnut spread, such as Nutella
100 g (3½ oz) milk chocolate, chopped or buttons
300 ml (10½ fl oz) pure (whipping) cream

To make the honey syrup, put all of the ingredients into a medium saucepan with 250 ml (9 fl oz/1 cup) of water. Bring to the boil over medium heat and boil for 3–4 minutes, until slightly reduced and syrupy.

Transfer to an airtight container and refrigerate until needed.

Put the warm water and yeast into the bowl of an electric mixer fitted with the whisk attachment and whisk on medium speed with a quarter of the flour. Once combined, remove from the mixer, cover with plastic wrap and set aside in a warm place for 30 minutes to froth up.

Return the bowl to the mixer and fit the paddle attachment, then beat on medium speed as you gradually add the remaining flour, sugar and vanilla paste. Beat until well combined, smooth and with no lumps.

Cover the bowl with plastic wrap again and set aside in a warm area for 1–1½ hours until the dough has doubled in size.

Meanwhile, make the chocolate dipping sauce. Put the chocolate spread and milk chocolate in a heatproof bowl and set aside.

In a small saucepan over medium heat, bring the cream to the boil, then pour it over the chocolate in the bowl. Stir until melted and completely combined. Reserve until needed – it can be served hot or cold.

Preheat the oil in a deep-fryer to 180°C (350°F) or in a deep-sided saucepan until a cube of bread dropped into the oil turns golden brown in 15 seconds.

Lightly grease hands with some cooking oil to prevent the dough sticking. Take a handful of dough and squeeze your hand into a fist to push out the dough out. Use a dessertspoon to scoop off a ball of dough and put it in the oil.

Deep-fry in batches, stirring in a circular motion for 2–3 minutes until the dough has puffed and has a nice golden colour.

Remove the loukoumades from the oil using a slotted spoon, and toss gently in the cold honey syrup.

Serve with the popcorn and chocolate dipping sauce in separate bowls.

MUM'S TWIST
Honestly I would recommend spending a session with a Greek giagiá to learn the technique of squeezing the dough, because it's a skill of its own.

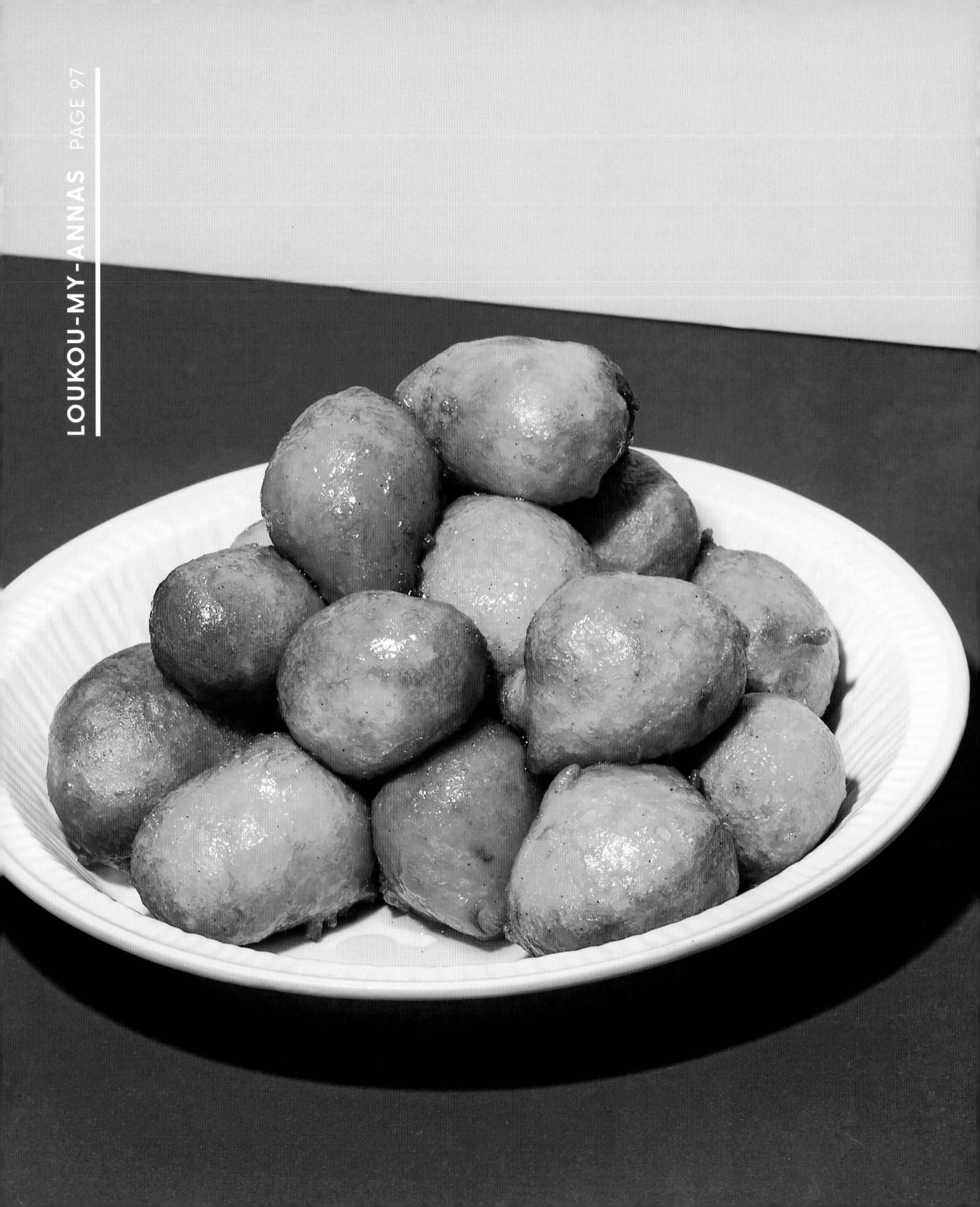

LOUKOU-MY-ANNAS PAGE 97

What Greek household doesn't make baklava? I love to take it apart layer by layer; that's the only way to eat it!

SERVES 20

375 g (13 oz) packet frozen filo pastry (about 20 sheets)
400 g (14 oz) unsalted butter, melted

SYRUP
495 g (1 lb 2 oz/2¼ cups) caster (superfine) sugar
30 ml (1 fl oz) honey
1 cinnamon stick
5 whole cloves
juice of 1 lemon juiced
1 vanilla bean, split

NUT MIXTURE
280 g (10 oz/1¾ cups) almonds with skin
110 g (3¾ oz/½ cup) caster (superfine) sugar
110 g (3¾ oz/1 cup) dry breadcrumbs
1 heaped tablespoon ground cinnamon

Put the syrup ingredients in a medium saucepan with 375 ml (13 fl oz/1½ cups) of water and bring to the boil. Remove from the heat and transfer to the refrigerator to chill until needed.

For the nut mixture, put the almonds in a food processor and process until coarsely chopped. Tip the almonds into a medium bowl and add the remaining ingredients. Mix well and set aside until needed.

Preheat the oven to 165°C (320°F). Lay the filo sheets on a clean work surface and cover with a clean tea towel (dish towel) that has been slightly dampened with cold water. This is to prevent the filo from drying out.

Brush some of the melted butter into a 20 x 30 x 4 cm (8 x 12 x 1½ inch) baking tin and lay 1 sheet of filo in the base. Brush with a little melted butter, then top with another filo sheet and lightly brush with melted butter. Repeat with another 3 filo sheets. Make sure the filo sheets slightly overhang the sides of the tin.

Scatter a small handful of the nut mixture evenly over the filo.

Continue layering 3 sheets of buttered filo then scattering the nut mixture on top until the tray is filled, finishing with 3 sheets of filo.

Use a small sharp knife to score the top of the baklava into triangles. Brush with the remaining melted butter and sprinkle a little water over the top. Bake for 1 hour or until golden and crisp.

While the dish is still hot, pour the cold syrup over it. Cut along the scored lines to serve triangles of baklava.

MUM'S TWIST
Make sure to score the filo before baking or you won't be able to cut it afterwards. Keep the syrup cold to add that crunch on the filo. Serve it with a glass of water and a cup of Greek coffee.

Mum only uses almonds; **she never liked** the smell of walnuts.

These potato doughnuts are my mother's recipe; it's one that will have you licking your fingertips and wanting more.

———

SERVES 12

———

2 kg (4 lb 8 oz/about 8) potatoes, unwashed
250 g (9 oz/1⅔ cups) self-raising flour
800 g (1 lb 12 oz) fine semolina
40 g (1½ oz) fresh yeast
375 ml (13 fl oz/1½ cups) warm water
vegetable oil, for deep-frying

SYRUP
1 kg (2 lb 4 oz) caster (superfine) sugar
1 teaspoon rosewater
10 whole cloves
juice of 1 lemon

———

Combine the sugar, rosewater and cloves with 750 ml (26 fl oz/3 cups) of water in a medium saucepan, and bring it to the boil over medium heat.

Remove from the heat and stir the lemon juice through, then transfer to a bowl and set aside in the refrigerator to chill.

Wash and peel the potatoes, put them into a steamer and steam until soft.

Transfer to a large bowl and mash well. Add in the flour, semolina and yeast with the warm water and mix well to combine.

Cover with a cloth and set aside for 30–45 minutes to rise like a bread dough.

Fill a piping (icing) bag fitted with a size 13 star nozzle. Heat the oil in a deep-fryer to 180°C (350°F) or in a deep-sided saucepan until a cube of bread dropped into the oil turns golden brown in 15 seconds.

Pipe the dough into the oil, using the scissors cut the dough into 5 cm (2 inch) lengths. Cook 2–3 at a time so as not to overcrowd the touloumbes.

When the touloumbes are golden brown and cooked through after about 5 minutes, remove them from the oil and carefully drop them into the cold syrup.

———

MUM'S TWIST
Use old potatoes with the dirt on them because they will have lost some of their water content and won't make the mixture too wet. To make sure the syrup stays cold, set the bowl in a larger bowl of iced water.

The mixture needs to rise: Mum used to say **you should allow it to sleep** and cover it with **a blanket.**

'Nouná' (pronounced noo-nah) is Greek for godmother, and I call mine 'noun' (pronounced like a short 'noon'). This haloumi is made using my nouná's recipe and it's priceless. Every time I'm in Melbourne, my mother gives me at least five kilograms (12 pounds) — I have no idea how much cheese she thinks I can eat, but it always gets eaten. As a cheese course or in a salad, its uses are endless.

SERVES 6

1 junket tablet (see glossary)
2 litres (70 fl oz/8 cups) unhomogenised milk
4 tablespoons salt
10–12 fresh mint leaves, finely chopped
lemon wedges, to serve

Dissolve the junket tablet in 1 tablespoon of water. Set aside.

In a medium saucepan over low heat, bring the milk to 32°C (90°F) — you'll need to use a thermometer. Remove from the heat, stir in the junket mixture and lay plastic wrap on the surface of the milk. Transfer to a warm place for 30 minutes or until a firm curd has formed.

Remove the plastic wrap and chop the curd into 2 cm (¾ inch) cubes. Make sure to cut all the way through the curd.

Rest the chopped curd for 5 minutes and return the saucepan to low heat. Raise the temperature to 35°C (95°F) and cook, stirring constantly, for 20 minutes, making sure the temperature is consistent. The cubes should look smooth and slightly elastic, forming a ricotta.

Remove from the heat and use a slotted spoon to transfer the ricotta into a colander lined with muslin (cheesecloth). Reserve the liquid to cook the haloumi with.

Cover the top of the ricotta with more cloth and add a weight on top. Set aside for 30 minutes.

Divide the haloumi mixture in half and form into oval shapes. Meanwhile, reheat the liquid (whey) in a small saucepan over medium heat until the mixture is 90°C (195°F).

Carefully add the haloumi pieces to the whey and cook, stirring regularly. The haloumi will rise to the surface. Allow to cook for a further 15 minutes.

Carefully remove the cheese from the whey and place on a tray to cool. Rub with sea salt. Lay half of the mint on the haloumi and fold the cheese in half. Allow to cool.

The cooled haloumi can be wrapped in plastic wrap and frozen or sliced immediately and pan-fried in a little olive oil to serve with lemon squeezed over it.

MUM'S TWIST
You can stop at the fresh ricotta stage and sprinkle ground cinnamon and a little sugar on top to make it sweet. When I do demos, I use haloumi as my cheese course with mini pita bread (see page 106), micro herbs and caramelised or fresh figs. I like to pan-fry the haloumi in front of my guests.

PITA

Dad's the man on the barbecue and Mum does the pita bread. We usually put haloumi and figs on the barbecue as well: they go together nicely.

MAKES 20

---

20 g (¾ oz) fresh yeast
250 ml (9 fl oz/1 cup) warm water
425 g (15 oz) plain (all-purpose) flour
2 teaspoons salt
1 tablespoon olive oil
sea salt and extra virgin olive oil, to serve

Combine the fresh yeast and warm water in a small bowl with 50 g (1¾ oz/⅓ cup) of the flour. Cover with plastic wrap and set aside in a warm place for 30 minutes.

In an electric mixer fitted with the dough hook attachment, combine the remaining flour and salt. Pour in the yeast mixture and beat on medium speed until a dough forms. Continue beating for 8–10 minutes while the dough develops and comes together. It should be smooth and elastic.

Spray a clean bowl with baking spray and turn the dough into the bowl. Cover with plastic wrap and set aside in a warm place for 1 hour or until the dough has doubled in size.

Preheat the oven to 230°C (450°F) and put a flat baking tray in the oven to heat.

Gently deflate the dough and turn it out onto a lightly floured work surface. Divide the dough into 20 pieces about 50 g (1¾ oz) each and form into balls. Cover with plastic wrap and set aside to rest for 10–15 minutes.

Use a floured rolling pin to roll out the balls of dough to discs 5 mm (¼ inch) thick and 7 cm (2¾ inches) diameter. Carefully remove the hot tray from the oven and sprinkle with flour. Lay the discs of dough on the tray with gaps between them.

Bake for 8–10 minutes or until puffed up and golden brown.

Remove from the oven and drizzle with olive oil and sea salt. Cover with a tea towel (dish towel) to keep warm if serving immediately.

MUM'S TWIST
Baking pita in a wood fire oven on direct heat is ideal. Make sure to prove the dough twice: you really need it to puff up so that it forms a pocket to fill with your favourite fillings.

Mum would **always say**, 'use **high heat** and it will **puff up like a football**'.

FILO

This filo recipe is ideally created for rolling up in the spanakopita. I used to go to my auntie's house just to eat her spanakopita. My favourite thing is the crunch of eating it warm, straight out of the oven.

————————

SERVES 6

————————

900 g (2 lb/6 cups) plain (all-purpose) flour, plus extra to dust
1 teaspoon salt
330 ml (11¼ fl oz/1⅓ cups) warm water, 50°C (120°F)
30 ml (1 fl oz) olive oil

————————

Combine the flour and salt in the bowl of an electric mixer fitted with the dough hook attachment. Add the water and mix on medium speed until the dough comes together.

Reduce the speed to low and add the oil, beating until combined. Stop the mixer and scrape down the side of the bowl, then beat on medium speed for 8–10 minutes, until the dough is smooth and elastic.

Turn the dough onto a lightly floured surface and roll it into a ball. Cover with plastic wrap and set aside to rest for 2 hours at room temperature.

Lay a clean 150 cm (59 inch) square cloth on a clean flat surface and dust the cloth with flour.

Place the dough in the centre of the cloth and use a floured rolling pin to roll the dough out to a 90 cm (35½ inch) square.

Using the backs of your hands, slide them underneath the pastry and stretch it gently, moving your hands to keep it even and working outwards from the centre to the edges.

Use your fingertips to give the edges a final stretch to make a 120 cm (47 inch) square. The pastry should be paper thin, so you can see through it.

Dust the top of the filo with flour and then roll the dough up in the cloth. Use the dough immediately, before it dries out, or freeze it for up to 1 week.

SPANAKOPITA

While the Aussie kids were eating Vegemite sandwiches, I would be embarrassed to unpack the spanakopita my mum had made. It's funny how things change: these days I'd be the coolest kid out.

————————

SERVES 8

————————

300 g (10½ oz) spinach or silverbeet (Swiss chard)
150 g (5½ oz) Greek feta cheese, crumbled
150 g (5½ oz) haloumi, grated
120 cm x 60 cm (47 inch x 24 inch) FILO pastry (left)
1 egg, beaten

————————

Preheat the oven to 170°C (325°F). Lightly grease an 18 cm (7 inch) round ovenproof pan.

To prepare the spinach, bring a saucepan of water to the boil. Add the spinach and cook for just 1 minute. Rinse the spinach under cold water until completely cool. Drain well, squeezing out as much excess water as possible.

In a medium bowl mix together the crumbled feta and the grated haloumi.

Lay the filo out on a clean cloth and brush evenly with the beaten egg. Season with a little pepper.

Spread three-quarters of the cheese mixture out on the filo, followed by the spinach.

Use the cloth to help you roll up the filo into a tight roulade. Cut off the ends of the log and roll the roulade into a loose spiral (snail) shape.

Transfer the spanakopita to the prepared pan and spread it out as much as you can so the sides of the roulade can cook too.

Brush with the remaining egg and scatter the remaining cheese over the top.

Bake for 1½ hours or until the filo is golden brown and crisp on the top and the bottom.

Serve warm or cold. Use scissors to cut the spanakopita into bite-size pieces

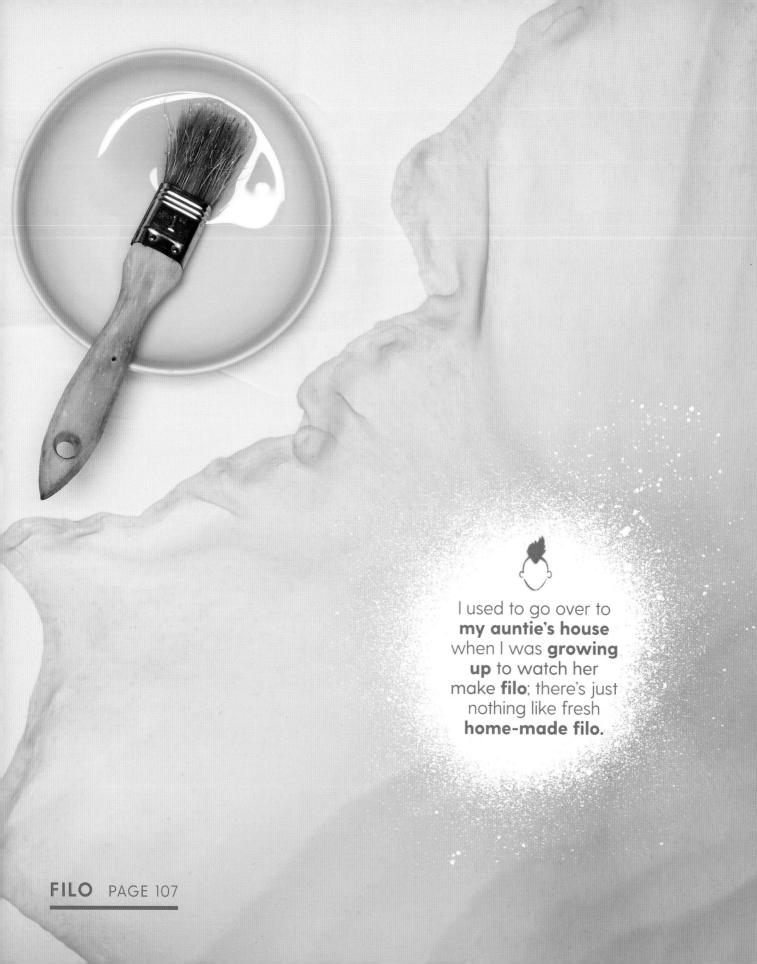

I used to go over to **my auntie's house** when I was **growing up** to watch her make **filo**; there's just nothing like fresh **home-made filo.**

FILO PAGE 107

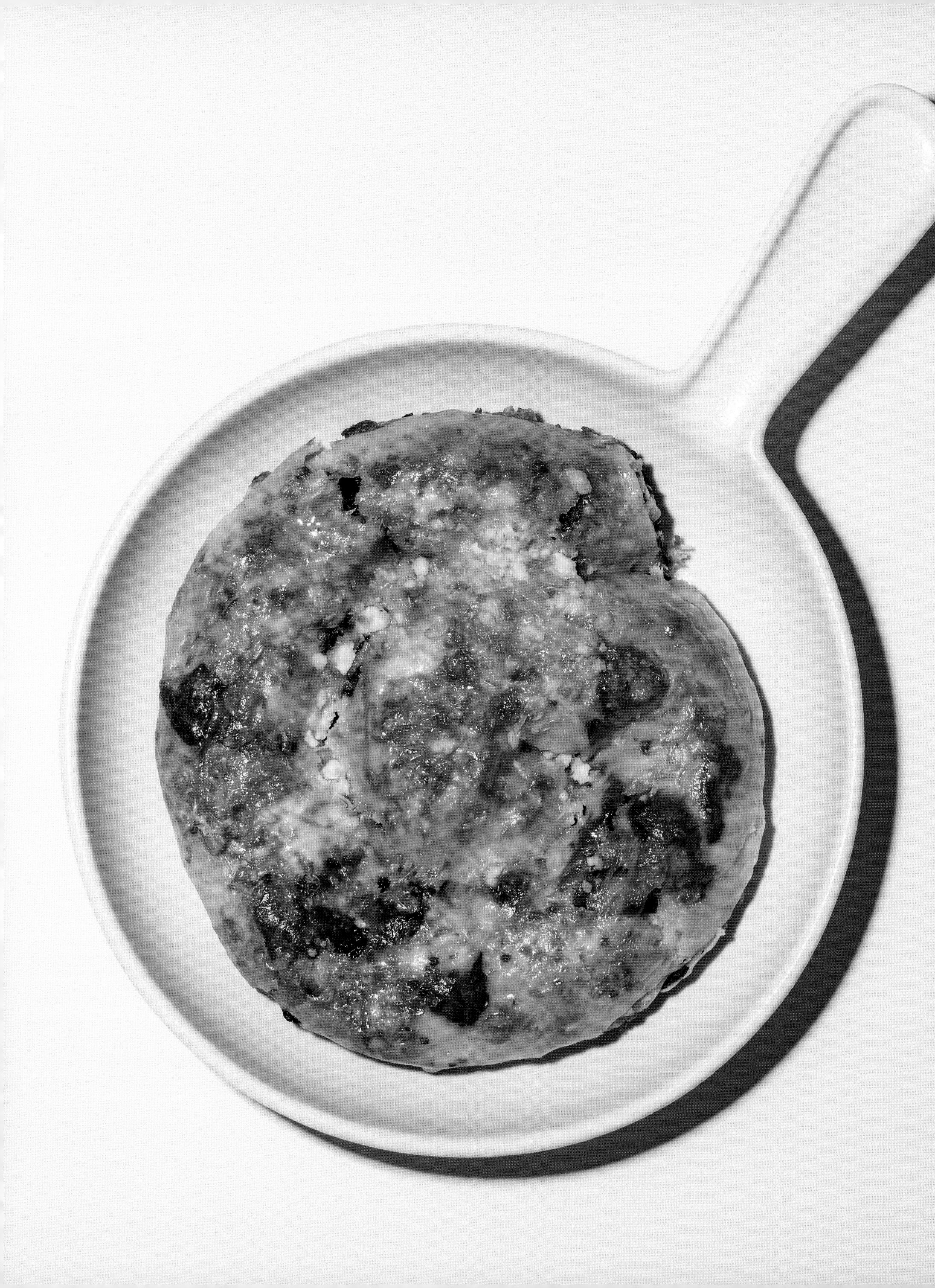

SPANAKOPITA PAGE 107

I believe that breakfast should be served at all times of the day. Granola is one of those foods that can be snacked on throughout the day. This recipe starts with Honey Nut Granola, which I bake into popsicles and serve with a yoghurt dipping sauce, or add a berry ripple sorbet with mix 'n' match fruit and other items.

I use this mixture for everything from dipping my chocolate lollipops for a function, breakfast, an ice-cream topping or just as a snack.

———

MAKES 1 kg (2 lb 4 oz)

———

250 g (9 oz/2½ cups) rolled oats
40 g (1½ oz/⅓ cup) desiccated (shredded) coconut
95 g (3¼ oz/¾ cup) slivered almonds
30 g (1 oz) raisins
30 g (1 oz) white sesame seeds
75 g (2¾ oz/½ cup) sunflower seeds
75 g (2¾ oz/½ cup) pepitas (pumpkin seeds)
35 g (1¼ oz) dried fruit mix
100 g (3½ oz/½ cup) light brown sugar
150 ml (5 fl oz) honey
70 ml (2¼ fl oz) vegetable oil
1 teaspoon vanilla bean paste

———

Preheat the oven to 160°C (315°F). Line a 24 x 32 cm (9½ x 12¾ inch) baking tray with baking paper.

Combine the oats, coconut, nuts and fruit in a large bowl, stirring to ensure it is well mixed.

In a medium saucepan, bring the sugar, honey, vegetable oil and vanilla bean paste to a slight simmer over medium heat, whisking until all ingredients are dissolved. Carefully pour the hot liquid over the granola mixture, then stir well to ensure the granola is coated evenly.

Transfer the mixture to the prepared tray, spreading it out so it bakes evenly.

Bake for 20–25 minutes, stirring the granola every 4–5 minutes so it cooks evenly. To test whether it is ready, place a small amount on the worktop to cool. It should be crunchy and toasted. If it's not, return it to the oven for 4–5 minutes before testing again.

Allow the granola to cool completely on the tray before transferring it to an airtight container. Store in the pantry for up to 3 weeks.

———

3SOME TWIST
This makes a wonderful gift for any occasion: present it in a jar with a label or add it to a Christmas hamper.

It's easy to change the nuts **and dried fruit,** especially if you need to **use up ingredients** in the **pantry.**

GRANOLA PADDLE-POP

Honey nut granola presented on a stick that can be dipped into natural yoghurt or simply served with fruit on top is a fun way to eat breakfast. I got new moulds shaped like a paddle-pop (popsicle/ice lolly) and wanted to see if I could bake in the moulds so the granola would hold its shape. If you don't have ovenproof paddle-pop moulds, you can use small muffin pans instead.

Note: Food grade paddle-pop sticks are available from cake decorating supply stores.

————

MAKES 10

————

HONEY NUT GRANOLA
125 g (4½ oz/1¼ cups) rolled oats
20 g (¾ oz/¼ cup) desiccated (shredded) coconut
45 g (1½ oz/½ cup) slivered almonds
2 tablespoons raisins
1½ tablespoons sunflower seeds
1½ tablespoons pepitas (pumpkin seeds)
1 tablespoon white sesame seeds
2 tablespoons mixed dried fruit
45 g (1½ oz/¼ cup lightly packed) light brown sugar
80 ml (2½ fl oz/⅓ cup) honey
2 tablespoons vegetable oil
1 teaspoon vanilla bean paste

YOGHURT MOUSSE
210 ml (7½ fl oz) milk
55 g (2 oz/¼ cup) caster (superfine) sugar
1 vanilla bean, split and seeds scraped
1 sheet titanium-strength gelatine, softened in cold water
845 g (1 lb 14 oz/3¼ cups) plain yoghurt
420 ml (14½ fl oz/1⅔ cups) pure (pouring) cream (35% fat), lightly whipped

————

Preheat the oven to 160°C (315°F). Lightly grease the moulds with cooking spray.

Combine the oats, coconut, nuts and fruit with a pinch of salt in a large bowl and stir to mix well.

In a medium saucepan, combine the sugar, honey, vegetable oil and vanilla. Bring to a slight simmer over medium heat, whisking until all ingredients have dissolved.

Carefully pour the hot syrup over the mixture in the bowl. Stir well so that the liquid evenly coats the granola mixture.

Divide the mixture between the paddle-pop moulds and insert the sticks, then bake for 40–45 minutes until golden brown. Remove from the oven and allow to cool completely before removing from the mould.

To make the yoghurt mousse, bring the milk, sugar and vanilla seeds to the boil in a small saucepan over medium heat. When the milk has just come to the boil, remove from the heat and whisk in the gelatine, squeezed gently to remove excess water. Allow to cool 40°C (105°F).

Meanwhile, put the yoghurt into a medium bowl. When the milk mixture has cooled, strain it through a fine sieve over the yoghurt and whisk until smooth.

Fold in the cream and then transfer to a serving bowl. Reserve in the refrigerator until needed.

To serve, choose 10 drinking glasses that are large enough for the paddle-pop to dip into. Divide the yoghurt mousse between the glasses, and lay a paddle-pop across the rim of each glass.

————

3SOME TWIST
Place the yoghurt mousse in a large glass bowl in the centre of the table and have the paddle-pops on the side so everyone can dip them in, for a little interaction between family and friends. Add a bit of extra flavour to the individual glasses: blitz up some fresh fruit and place it on top of the yoghurt mousse so you can spoon into it with the paddle pop. You can skip the yoghurt mousse and just use plain or flavoured yoghurt.

This blueberry yoghurt sorbet is one of my favourites, using Greek yoghurt and a little bit of olive oil. The combination brings out a fresh, comforting taste that will add a delicious something extra to your breakfast bowl.

SERVES 8

1 quantity HONEY NUT GRANOLA (see page 113)
250 g (9 oz) strawberries, hulled and halved
150 g (5½ oz) raspberries
150 g (5½ oz) blueberries
4 peaches, stone removed, cut into wedges
4 figs, quartered
desiccated (shredded) coconut, for serving

BLUEBERRY YOGHURT SORBET
50 g (1¾ oz) frozen blueberries
125 g (4½ oz) caster (superfine) sugar
2 teaspoons lemon juice
160 g (5¾ oz) Greek-style yoghurt
50 ml (1¾ fl oz) olive oil

Make blueberry jam by putting the blueberries and 1 tablespoon of caster sugar in a small saucepan and bring to the boil. Simmer over low heat for 15–20 minutes; make sure to stir so it does not catch. Set aside to cool.

In a small saucepan, combine the remaining caster sugar with 80 ml (2½ fl oz/⅓ cup) of water and bring to the boil, then remove from the heat and allow to cool completely. Stir in the lemon juice.

Put the yoghurt into a mixing bowl. Gradually add the cooled syrup, whisking constantly until it is all combined.

Gradually whisk in the oil until combined.

Pour the mixture into an ice-cream machine and churn the sorbet to the correct frozen consistency.

When the sorbet is ready, slowly fold in the blueberry jam to create a ripple effect. Reserve leftover jam for serving.

Transfer to a stainless steel bowl and cover with baking paper or plastic wrap. Freeze until needed.

To serve, put the granola, fruit, leftover jam and some coconut into separate bowls and arrange them on a board or tray in the centre of the table.

Quenelle the sorbet and divide between eight serving bowls. Allow your guests to mix 'n' match their own toppings.

3SOME TWIST
The variety of this dish is endless: the main components are the sorbet and granola. Serve them with your choice of fruits and other toppings. If you don't have an ice-cream churn, use ready-made sorbet. Serve it with milk to soften the granola, if desired.

ROCKSTAR = HIGH MAINTENANCE. Many of the recipes in this chapter are star desserts that have featured on television and people have gone crazy for them. There are a lot of steps, so take a few days to make all of the separate elements and assemble them on the day of serving.

When I was first asked to go on *MasterChef Australia* I really tried to get Anna's Mess on, because I thought it looked so beautiful and elegant. The second time I was invited on the show they allowed me to actually drop it. From a small dessert, it went large; from a tap with a spoon it went to dropping from great heights. The dessert went viral, not only in Australia, but around the world. A year later it had so many views – in the millions – that we had people who travelled around the world just to eat it. Remember, the only way to eat Anna's Mess is to create a mess.

Note: for this recipe you will need some specialty equipment. Two 13 cm (5 inch) and one 7 cm (2¾ inch) sphere chocolate moulds; a piping (icing) bag and size 9 plain nozzle; a sugar thermometer; an airless spray gun; a small test tube.

――――――――

SERVES 2

――――――――

MERINGUE KISSES
3½ egg whites
100 g (3½ oz) caster (superfine) sugar
50 g (1¾ oz) pure icing (confectioners') sugar, sifted

Preheat the oven to 74°C (165°F) and line a baking tray with baking paper.

Use an electric mixer fitted with the whisk attachment to whisk the egg whites on high speed in a clean dry bowl until soft peaks form. Reduce the speed and gradually add the caster sugar.

Return the mixer to high speed and whisk until the meringue is thick and glossy and the sugar has dissolved. Rub a little meringue between your fingers; if it feels gritty, continue to whisk. Firm peaks need to be achieved. This should take about 5 minutes.

Remove the bowl from the mixer and quickly fold in the icing sugar, or the meringue will become runny.

Using a piping (icing) bag fitted with a size 9 plain nozzle, pipe the meringue onto the prepared trays and bake for 2½ hours or until dried out. Keep

checking to make sure the temperature isn't too high as no colour is wanted. Remove from the oven and allow to cool on the trays, then store in an airtight container until required. They will keep for 1–2 weeks.

――――――――

RASPBERRY FINANCIER SPONGE
60 g (2¼ oz) unsalted butter
25 g (1 oz) plain (all-purpose) flour, sifted
25 g (1 oz/¼ cup) almond meal, sifted
2 egg whites
60 g (2¼ oz) caster (superfine) sugar
6 fresh raspberries, halved

Heat the butter in a small saucepan over medium heat. Whisk the butter as it melts, then stop whisking and allow the butter to cook until lightly browned specks form in the butter and there is a nutty aroma. Keep a close eye on it as the butter can easily burn.

Remove the pan from the heat and pass the butter through a sieve into a medium bowl. Put it into the refrigerator to cool.

Preheat the oven to 160°C (315°F). Line a baking tray with baking paper. Grease a 9 cm (3½ inch) diameter baking ring with cooking oil and line with baking paper.

Combine the flour and almond meal in a bowl.

Put the egg whites and sugar in the bowl of an electric mixer fitted with the whisk attachment. Whisk until firm peaks form. When the meringue has reached firm peak, remove the bowl from the machine and fold in the flour and almond mixture.

Fold about half of the almond meringue mixture into the cooled butter, until well combined. Now fold this mixture back into the almond meringue mixture until smooth and well combined.

Gently fold the raspberries into the financier mixture, being careful not to break up the raspberries. Pour the financier mixture into the prepared ring and bake for 8–12 minutes until golden brown and the sponge springs back when gently pressed. Carefully remove the sponge from the ring to avoid the sponge shrinking from the side. Set aside to cool until needed for assembly.

――――――――

STRAWBERRY COULIS

250 ml (9 fl oz/1 cup) strawberry purée (see
    glossary)
65 g (2½ oz) pure icing (confectioners') sugar, sifted

In a small saucepan, bring the strawberry purée just
to the boil over medium heat. Make sure it doesn't boil,
as it will lose the fresh flavour. Remove from the heat.

Whisk in the icing sugar and return to medium
heat. Use a whisk to stir constantly until the icing
sugar has dissolved.

Remove the pan from the heat, pass the coulis
through a sieve and carefully pour the coulis into a
deep tray. Cover the surface with plastic wrap and
put it into the refrigerator to cool. Reserve until
needed for assembly.

CARA CRUNCH INSERT

75 g (2¾ oz) dark chocolate (53%), chopped or
    buttons
50 g (1¾ oz) Cara Crakine™ (caramel chocolate
    crunch filling)
25 g (1 oz) black sesame seeds

Put the dark chocolate and Cara Crakine in a
microwave-proof bowl. Microwave for 30 seconds
at a time, stirring after each burst, until completely
melted. Mix in the black sesame seeds until combined.

Lay a 20 x 30 cm (8 x 12 inch) piece of baking
paper onto a flat work surface and pour the melted
chocolate on. Lay another piece of baking paper on
top and roll out the mixture with a rolling pin until
5 mm (¼ inch) thick.

Lay it on a flat tray and stand it in the refrigerator
for 30 minutes or until set solid.

Remove from the refrigerator and cut out a 9 cm
(3½ inch) disc. Reserve the disc in the refrigerator until
needed for assembly.

RASPBERRY CURD

4 eggs
220 g (7¾ oz/1 cup) caster (superfine) sugar
200 ml (7 fl oz) raspberry purée (see glossary)
2½ sheets titanium-strength gelatine, softened
    in iced water
70 g (2½ oz) butter

Whisk the eggs and sugar together in a bowl until
well combined. Set aside.

In a medium saucepan, bring the raspberry purée
to the boil over medium heat. Carefully pour the
boiling purée onto the egg mixture and whisk well.
Return the mixture to the saucepan, making sure to
scrape out all of the mixture and whisk together.

Cook over high heat, whisking constantly, until
the mixture reaches 86°C (187°F) on a sugar
thermometer. When it has reached the required
temperature, remove from the heat and stir in the
softened gelatine until completely dissolved.

Strain the curd through a fine sieve into a deep
tray and allow to cool to 40°C (104°F).

Stand a 7 cm (2¾ inch) silicone sphere mould
on a flat tray. Blend in the butter and fill the mould
halfway with 60 g (2¼ oz) of curd. Transfer to the
freezer until set.

MASCARPONE AND VANILLA MOUSSE

60 ml (2 fl oz/¼ cup) milk
2 vanilla beans, split and seeds scraped
1½ egg yolks
30 g (1 oz) caster (superfine) sugar
1½ sheets titanium-strength gelatine, softened
80 g (2¾ oz) white chocolate (53%), chopped
    or buttons
100 g (3½ oz) mascarpone
125 ml (4 fl oz/½ cup) pure (pouring) cream (35% fat),
    lightly whisked

In a small saucepan, put the milk, vanilla beans and
seeds and bring to the boil over medium–high heat.

Meanwhile, whisk the egg yolks and caster sugar
together in a medium bowl, until completely combined.

CONTINUED >>

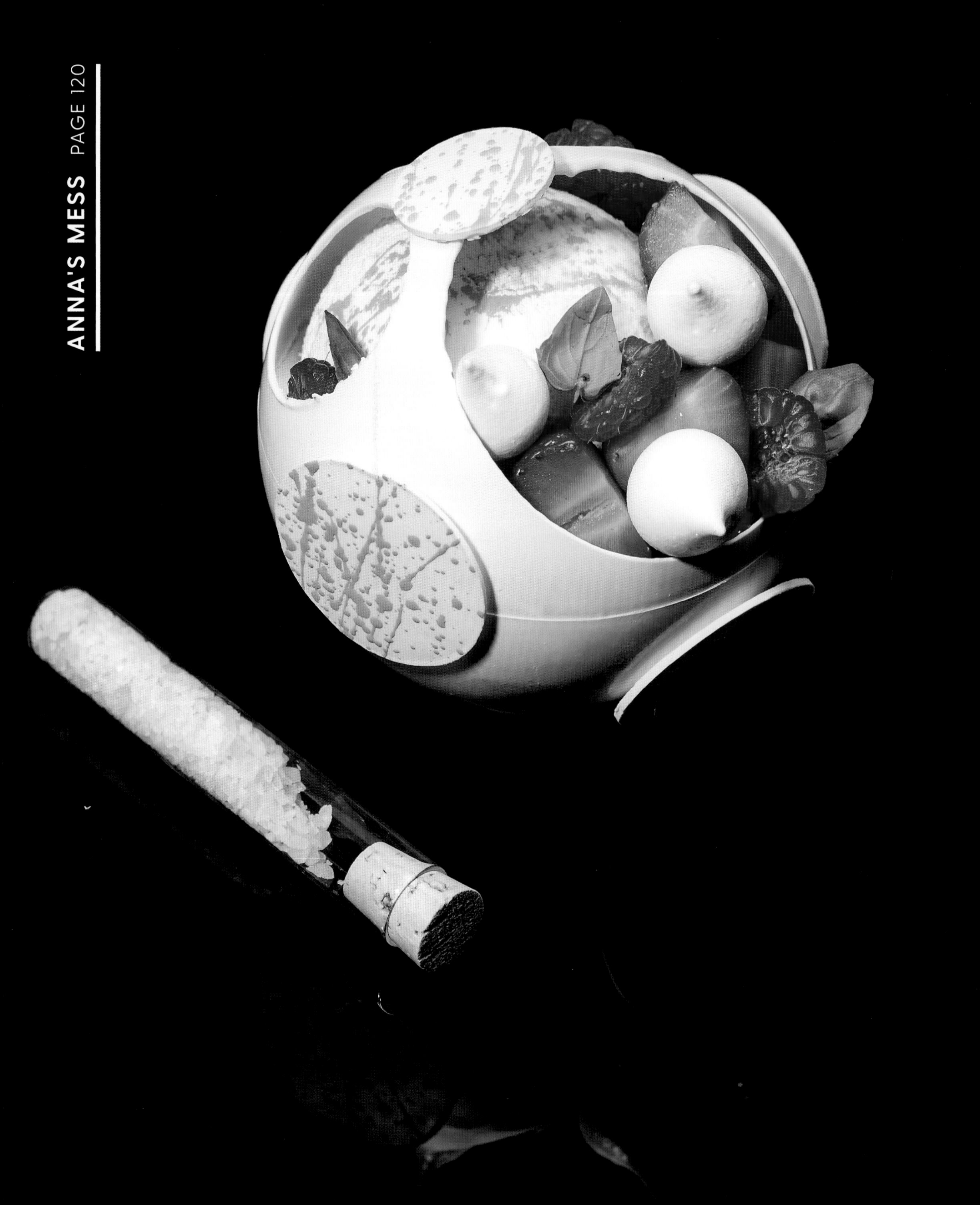

ANNA'S MESS PAGE 120

Pour the hot milk mixture onto the egg mixture and whisk well. Return the egg and milk mixture to the saucepan, making sure to scrape out all the mixture, and whisk together.

Return the saucepan to medium heat and use a spatula to stir constantly. Cook until the crème anglaise reaches 86°C (187°F) or until it thickly coats the back of a spoon.

Take the saucepan off the heat, remove the vanilla beans and whisk in the softened gelatine. Put the white chocolate into a medium bowl, then pass the custard through a fine sieve onto the chocolate. Whisk together until completely melted and combined.

Cover the surface of the crème anglaise with plastic wrap and reserve in the refrigerator (to stop it cooking further) until ready to assemble the bottom dome.

Reserve the mascarpone and cream separately until ready to assemble the bottom dome.

WHITE CHOCOLATE DOMES AND SHAPES
1.5 kg (3 lb 5 oz) white chocolate (53%), chopped or buttons
100 g (3½ oz) cocoa butter
30 g (1 oz) titanium dioxide (white) colouring powder (optional) (see glossary)

In a microwave-proof bowl, melt 1 kg (2 lb 4 oz) of white chocolate in 40-second bursts, stirring after each burst, until three-quarters of the chocolate is melted and smooth. Remove from the microwave and stir until all of the chocolate is combined and smooth.

Whisk the remaining white chocolate into the melted chocolate in three batches. The chocolate will become cool and still have lumps in it.

Meanwhile, heat the cocoa butter in a microwave-proof bowl in 40-second bursts until completely melted.

Stir the white colouring powder into the cocoa butter and then use a handheld blender to blend until combined. Strain through a fine sieve. Pour the white cocoa butter into the white chocolate and use the handheld blender to combine.

Temper the chocolate to 28–29°C (82–84°F) following the instructions on page 232. Meanwhile polish the sphere chocolate moulds with cotton balls

to ensure they are shiny and clean. Fill the polished moulds with the chocolate and ensure the entire surface is covered.

Turn the moulds over and tap out the excess chocolate, scraping down the chocolate. Stand on a piece of baking paper to set.

Spread the excess chocolate as evenly and thinly as possible onto a piece of acetate. Allow to set until firm, but not hard, then cut out one 12 cm (4½ inch) disc, two 3 cm (1¼ cm) discs, two 5 cm (2 inch) discs and two 5.5 cm (2¼ inch) discs. To flatten, lay the discs on a tray lined with baking paper and lay a second sheet of baking paper on top of the discs and then a dry tray flat on top. Transfer the trays to the refrigerator until ready to assemble.

When the chocolate in the sphere moulds has set, carefully remove the moulds from the baking paper and leave them in the refrigerator for 5–10 minutes.

When ready to assemble, carefully remove the chocolate domes from the moulds: do not hit the mould on the work surface as the chocolate dome will break. Reserve one of the domes for the top and place the other dome on a stand to assemble the bottom of Anna's Mess.

TO ASSEMBLE THE BASE
Pour 100 g (3½ oz) of strawberry coulis into the bottom of the dome, making sure not to drip on the sides of the dome. Place the 9 cm (3½ inch) Cara Crunch disc on top of the coulis and then the Raspberry Financier Sponge.

To finish off the mascarpone mousse, the crème anglaise needs to be at 40°C (105°F), therefore it may need to be carefully heated in the microwave in 30 second bursts, stirring between each burst. Whisk the crème anglaise to make sure it is smooth.

When the crème anglaise is the right temperature, fold in the mascarpone and then the whipped cream. Pour the mascarpone mousse into the bottom dome to fill it up to the top, but not overflowing.

Stand the bottom dome on a flat tray and transfer to the refrigerator to set.

WHITE TITANIUM SPRAY

100 g (3½ oz) cocoa butter
10 g (⅜ oz) titanium dioxide (white) colouring powder

Put the cocoa butter in a microwave-proof bowl and heat in 40-second bursts, stirring between each one, until completely melted.

Stir in the titanium colouring powder and blend with a handheld blender until combined. Strain thought a fine sieve.

Cool the coloured cocoa butter down to 34°C (93°F).

Set up the spray gun according to the manufacturer's instructions and line a baking tray with baking paper. Unmould the raspberry curd dome onto the tray and put it into the freezer for 5 minutes until solid.

Spray the raspberry curd dome with white cocoa butter. Make sure to cover the whole dome, but don't add too much colour. Return to the freezer until ready to add the graffiti.

PINK CHOCOLATE GRAFFITI

30 g (1 oz) pink chocolate colouring

Remove the lid of the bottle of pink colouring into the microwave and heat in 30-second bursts, shaking the bottle between each burst, until the colour has melted.

Pour the melted colouring into a small clean bowl. Set aside until it has cooled down to 34°C (93°).

Remove the raspberry curd dome from the freezer and use a pastry brush to flick the cooled pink colouring over the dome. Return the dome to the freezer until ready to assemble the dessert.

To graffiti the white chocolate discs, place one each of the 3 cm (1¼ inch), 5 cm (2 inch) and 5.5 cm (2¼ inch) chocolate discs on a baking tray lined with baking paper and use the same pastry brush to flick the pink colour on. Allow to dry and then reserve until ready to assemble.

TO ASSEMBLE THE TOP

125 g (4½ oz) fresh strawberries, hulled and halved
75 g (2¾ oz) fresh raspberries, halved
1 small handful of basil leaves, washed
20 g (¾ oz) white chocolate
pop rocks (see glossary) in small test tubes

Stand the bottom dome on a serving plate, using the chocolate stand to keep it steady. Place the 12 cm (4½ inch) white chocolate disc on the mascarpone mousse and then place the raspberry curd dome on the chocolate disc.

Place 4 strawberry halves on the dessert, followed by 5 raspberry halves, 8 meringue kisses and 4 basil leaves.

To cut a hole in the top chocolate dome, heat an 8.5 cm (3⅜ inch) metal circle cutter with a blowtorch and carefully press into the chocolate. Repeat to cut a hole with a 6 cm (2½ inch) metal circle cutter and then again with a 5.5 cm (2¼ inch) metal circle cutter. Space the holes evenly around the chocolate dome.

Place the top dome over the garnished bottom dome, making sure all the toppings are contained within the sphere.

Melt the white chocolate and fill a small piping bag. Pipe a little dot onto the back of each of the chocolate discs and stick the discs onto the outside of Anna's Mess. Serve with a test tube of pop rocks.

ROCKSTAR TWIST

Make each of the components of Anna's Mess separately over a few days. Be sure to temper the chocolate well, otherwise it will crack or melt and not hold together.

My Carrot Cake won the prize for best dessert in Australia in 2014, then in 2015 *MasterChef Australia* called me and asked for it to be one of the challenges. With 1.2 million viewers, I was a household name the next day. At the Shangri-La hotel in Sydney, there were queues out to the street! As a result, and thanks to Matt Preston, I became known as the Punk Princess of Pastry.

SERVES 4

APRICOT AND CARROT SORBET

30 ml (1 fl oz) glucose syrup
90 g (3¼ oz) caster (superfine) sugar
½ teaspoon sorbet stabiliser (see glossary)
1 tablespoon lemon juice
200 ml (7 fl oz) apricot purée (see glossary)
100 ml (3½ fl oz) carrot juice

Combine the glucose syrup and 70 ml (2¼ fl oz) water in a small saucepan. Mix together the sugar and sorbet stabiliser, add to the saucepan and bring to the boil over high heat. Set aside.

Combine the lemon juice, apricot purée and carrot juice in a medium bowl.

Pour the hot syrup into the juice mixture and whisk until combined. Strain into a clean bowl set over a larger bowl of iced water to cool.

Churn in an ice-cream machine according to the manufacturer's instructions. Set aside in the freezer until needed.

CARROT CAKE

50g (1¾ oz/⅓ cup) plain (all-purpose) flour
40 g (1½ oz) brown sugar
2 pinches of bicarbonate of soda (baking soda)
2 pinches of baking powder
1 egg, lightly beaten
30 ml (1 fl oz) vegetable oil
2 pinches of ground cinnamon
1 carrot, peeled and grated
1 green apple, peeled and grated
1 tablespoon coarsely chopped walnuts
2 tablespoons sultanas (golden raisins)

Preheat the oven to 160°C (315°F) and lightly grease four 8 cm (3¼ inch) diameter baking rings.

Put the flour, brown sugar, bicarbonate of soda, baking powder and a pinch of salt in a medium bowl and stir to combine.

Gradually add the egg and oil and beat until combined into a smooth mixture.

Add the remaining ingredients and stir until they all just come together.

Divide the mixture evenly among the prepared rings and bake for 15–18 minutes, until a skewer inserted into the centre comes out clean. Remove the cakes from the oven and transfer to the freezer for 2 hours.

When frozen, slice the cakes horizontally into 5 mm (¼ inch) thick rounds. Use a 6 cm (2½ inch) round cutter to cut out discs and return them to the freezer. Reserve the outer rings of the cake for the CARROT CAKE CRUMBLE (see opposite page).

APRICOT AND CARROT INSERT

70 ml (2¼ fl oz) apricot purée (see glossary)
2 teaspoons caster (superfine) sugar
1 sheet titanium-strength gelatine, softened in cold water
2 tablespoons carrot juice

Warm the apricot purée and sugar in a small saucepan over medium heat until the sugar has dissolved, but do not let the mixture boil. Remove from the heat.

Add the softened gelatine and carrot juice and stir until dissolved. Pass the mixture through a fine sieve.

Pour 3 teaspoons (15 ml/½ fl oz) of the mixture into four 6 cm (2½ inch) round silicone moulds and freeze until needed for assembly.

CRUNCH DISC

20 g (¾ oz) Venezuela dark chocolate (72%), chopped or buttons
100 g (3½ oz) hazelnut praline paste (see glossary)
1½ tablespoons puffed rice (Rice Bubbles, Rice Krispies or similar)
1½ tablespoons pailleté feuilletine (see glossary)

Melt the dark chocolate in a microwave-proof bowl in bursts of 15 seconds, stirring between each burst, so the chocolate does not burn.

Stir in the hazelnut praline paste until well combined and smooth. Fold in the puffed rice and pailleté feuilletine until combined.

Roll gently between two pieces of baking paper; avoid breaking the puffed rice in the mixture. Roll to 3 mm (⅛ inch) thickness. Transfer to a tray and freeze.

Remove the crunch sheet from the freezer and cut out four discs using a 6 cm (2½ inch) round cutter. Return to the freezer.

CARROT CAKE CRUMBLE

Preheat the oven to 140°C (275°F) and line a baking tray with baking paper.

Crumble the carrot cake scraps onto the tray and bake for 1–2 hours until dried out. Cool on the tray.

Transfer to a food processor and process to form crumbs. Set aside.

PRALINE CREMEUX

60 ml (2 fl oz/¼ cup) milk
185 ml (6 fl oz/¾ cup) pure (pouring) cream (35% fat)
¼ vanilla bean, split and seeds scraped
2 tablespoons caster (superfine) sugar
2 egg yolks
2 teaspoons cornflour (cornstarch)
½ sheet titanium-strength gelatine, softened in cold water
100 g (3½ oz) hazelnut praline paste (see glossary)

Combine the milk, 60 ml (2 fl oz/¼ cup) of the cream and the vanilla bean and seeds in a small saucepan over medium heat.

Meanwhile, whisk together the sugar and egg yolks in a bowl until creamy. Add the cornflour and whisk until combined.

When the milk and cream has come to the boil, remove from the heat and add a little to the egg mixture. Whisk together and then pour the egg mixture into the saucepan and continue to whisk.

Return to the heat and cook for 4 minutes or until it has a custard consistency. Remove from the heat and whisk in the softened gelatine. Pass through a sieve, then whisk in the hazelnut praline paste. Allow the mixture to cool to 40°C (104°F) or just above body temperature.

Whisk the remaining cream until semi-whipped. Fold the cream into the hazelnut mixture. Transfer the mixture to a piping (icing) bag.

ASSEMBLE THE CAKE

Line the inside of four 8 cm (3¼ inch) round moulds with strips of acetate. Place on a small tray lined with baking paper. Pipe a layer of praline cremeux into the moulds until just under halfway up the side.

Remove the apricot and carrot inserts from the moulds and set them into the middle of the cremeux, with the bigger surface area facing up. Push the insert into the cremeux gently.

Place a crunch disc on top of each insert, followed by a disc of the carrot cake, pressing down gently between each layer.

Transfer to the freezer for 2–3 hours until completely firm.

CONTINUED >>

Putting a whole **new spin** on the taste and look of **carrot cakes.** I take what **people know and like**, and give it a new **cool, fun twist.**

CARROT CAKE PAGE 126

CARAMEL GLAZE

150 ml (5 fl oz) pure (pouring) cream (35% fat)
¼ vanilla bean, split and seeds scraped
190 g (6¾ oz) caster (superfine) sugar
1½ tablespoons cornflour (cornstarch)
35 g (1¼ oz) white chocolate, chopped or buttons
2½ sheets titanium-strength gelatine, softened in
    cold water

Put the cream and vanilla bean and seeds in a small saucepan and bring to the boil. Discard vanilla bean.

Meanwhile, combine 175 g (6 oz) of the sugar in a saucepan with 140 ml (4¾ fl oz) of water over medium heat, stirring until sugar just dissolves.

Using a thermometer, cook the mixture until it reaches 204°C (405°F) and turns caramel in colour. Whisking constantly, pour the boiled cream over the caramel.

Combine the remaining caster sugar and cornflour in a bowl and add 1 tablespoon of water, stirring to make a paste. Add the paste to the caramel mixture.

Bring the caramel mixture back to the boil and continue cooking, whisking constantly, for a few more minutes, until thickened.

Put the white chocolate in a heatproof bowl, pour the caramel mixture over and stir until the chocolate is melted and the mixture is smooth. Add the softened gelatine and stir until dissolved.

Strain into a jug and cover the surface with plastic wrap. Set aside until ready to glaze the carrot cake.

CREAM CHEESE FOAM

100 ml (3½ fl oz) milk
200 ml (7 fl oz) pure (pouring) cream (35% fat)
2 egg yolks
2 tablespoons caster (superfine) sugar
100 g (3½ oz) cream cheese

Put the milk and 150 ml (5 fl oz) of the cream in a small saucepan and heat until just beginning to bubble.

Meanwhile, put the egg yolks and sugar into a bowl and whisk to combine. While constantly whisking, slowly add the hot milk mixture to the egg mixture. Return the mixture to the saucepan and set over medium heat. Cook, stirring constantly, until the mixture coats the back of a spoon. Remove from the heat and strain into a bowl. Sit this bowl in a larger bowl of iced water to cool the anglaise mixture.

Combine the cream cheese and the remaining cream in a saucepan over medium heat, stirring until soft.

Add 100 g (3½ oz) of the reserved, cooled anglaise and blend until combined. Set aside over a bowl of iced water.

When cool, transfer the cream cheese mixture to a whipped cream siphon (see glossary), charge the siphon twice according to the manufacturer's instructions and lay the siphon on its side in the refrigerator until needed.

CARAMELISED WALNUT CRUMBLE

150 g (5½ oz/1⅓ cups) walnuts
110 g (3¾ oz/½ cup) caster (superfine) sugar

Spread the walnuts on a baking tray lined with baking paper.

Put the sugar into a saucepan with 60 ml (2 fl oz/¼ cup) of water over medium heat. Cook, brushing down the side of the saucepan with water as necessary, until the sugar has dissolved and caramelised.

Pour the caramel over the walnuts and set aside until hard. Coarsely chop the walnut caramel and set aside.

CANDY CARROT STRIPS

1 carrot
110 g (3¾ oz/½ cup) caster (superfine) sugar

Use a vegetable peeler to peel the carrot into long strips.

Combine 100 ml (3½ fl oz) of water and the sugar in a small saucepan and bring to the boil.

Remove from the heat and add the carrot strips. Cover with a cartouche (see glossary) and set aside to cool.

――――――

YELLOW CHOCOLATE GRAFFITI MIXTURE

50 g (1¾ oz) cocoa butter
2 teaspoons titanium white food colouring powder
yellow food colouring

Put the cocoa butter in a microwave-proof bowl and heat in 40-second bursts, stirring between each burst, until completely melted.

Stir in the titanium food colouring powder and blend until combined. Strain through a fine sieve into a small bowl.

Slowly add the yellow colour until you are happy with the shade. Cool the mixture to 34°C (93°F) or just below body temperature.

――――――

CHOCOLATE DISCS

200 g (7 oz) milk chocolate, tempered
    (see page 232)
200 g (7 oz) orange coloured and flavoured
    chocolate, tempered (see page 232)

Spread the tempered milk chocolate as evenly and thinly as possible on a sheet of acetate. Allow to set until firm, but not hard. Cut out discs using 3 cm (1¼ inch) and 4 cm (1½ inch) round cutters. You'll need four discs of each size (one of each for each cake).

Spread the tempered orange chocolate as evenly and thinly as possible on a sheet of acetate. Allow to set until firm, but not hard. Cut out discs using a 3 cm (1¼ inch) round cutter. You'll need four discs (one for each cake).

Lay baking paper on top of the discs and put a flat tray on top. Keep in the refrigerator until ready for assembly.

――――――

PLATE UP

1 small handful of baby celery leaves, trimmed

Reheat the caramel glaze to 40°C (104°F) and the yellow chocolate graffiti mixture to 34°C (93°F).

Remove the cake from the freezer and set on a wire rack over a tray to catch drips. Pour over the warmed glaze until the cake is completely covered.

Using a clean dry pastry brush, spatter the chocolate graffiti mixture on one side of the cake.

Carefully transfer the cake to a presentation platter.

Scatter carrot cake crumbs, caramelised walnut crumble and carrot ribbons around the base of the cake. Press the large and small milk chocolate discs and the orange chocolate disc into the cake on one side.

Add a squirt of cream cheese foam to the other side of the serving plate.

Place a teaspoon quenelle of sorbet on top and scatter baby celery leaves to garnish.

――――――

ROCKSTAR TWIST

Take your time when plating up to make sure everything is placed correctly so it doesn't look like a mess. The glaze needs to be at the right temperature so that it's thin and glossy. The yellow graffiti mixture also should be just the correct temperature or the colour will run and you'll lose the graffiti look.

I designed this birthday cake for my partner of 10 years, Casey, and I named it after her too. I wanted to make a priceless and romantic gesture, so it contains all of her favourite flavours: banana, caramel, passionfruit. It has macarons and graffiti for an additional 'wow' factor.

SERVES 4–6

BANANA BREAD
100 g (3½ oz) caster (superfine) sugar
100 g (3½ oz) ripe bananas
1 egg
2 tablespoons milk
30 ml (1 fl oz) vegetable oil
100 g (3½ oz/⅔ cup) plain (all purpose) flour
½ teaspoon salt
1 teaspoon baking powder

Preheat the oven to 160°C (315°F). Set an 18 cm (7 inch) cake ring with a removable base and a 6 x 9 x 4 cm (2½ x 3½ x 1½ inch) mini loaf (bar) tin on a baking tray. Spray both very well with baking spray and set aside.

In an electric mixer fitted with the whisk attachment, whisk the sugar and banana on medium speed for a few minutes until the bananas are broken down.

Reduce to low speed and add the egg, milk and oil, bit by bit, making sure the liquids have combined completely before adding the next amount.

Sift the dry ingredients twice and slowly add to the banana mixture, while still whisking.

Pour the banana bread mixture into the round cake tin to a depth of about 1 cm (⅜ inch), then pour the remaining mix into the mini loaf tin.

Bake for 30–35 minutes until a skewer comes out clean and the bread springs back when pressed.

Remove from the oven and cool for 10 minutes in the tin. Carefully turn out of the tins onto a wire rack to cool completely.

MILK CHOCOLATE CRUNCH
100 g (3½ oz) milk chocolate, chopped or buttons
50 g (1¾ oz) pailleté feuilletine (see glossary)

In a microwave-proof bowl, melt the milk chocolate in 30-second bursts, stirring between each burst until smooth. Fold the pailleté feuilletine through.

Evenly spread the crunch mixture onto the cooled banana bread disc. Transfer to a baking tray and put it in the refrigerator to set.

When the chocolate crunch has set, trim the cake to a 16 cm (6¼ inch) disc and cut out the centre using a 7 cm (2¾ inch) round cutter, forming a ring. Transfer to a tray in the refrigerator and reserve until needed.

PASSIONFRUIT CURD
80 ml (2½ fl oz/⅓ cup) passionfruit purée (see glossary)
1 tablespoon lemon juice
2 eggs
110 g (3¾ oz/½ cup) caster (superfine) sugar
2 sheets titanium-strength gelatine, softened in cold water
150 g (5½ oz) unsalted butter

Combine the passionfruit purée and lemon juice in a small saucepan over high heat. Bring to the boil.

Meanwhile, whisk the eggs and sugar in a heatproof bowl until well combined.

Pour the boiling juice mixture into the egg mixture. Whisk together, then pour back into the saucepan and return to the stovetop over medium heat. Continue whisking as you heat the curd to 84°C (183°F) using a thermometer.

Remove from the heat and whisk in the softened gelatine. Strain into a deep tray and allow to cool to 40°C (104°F).

Blend in the butter, then measure 200 g (7 oz) into a piping (icing) bag fitted with a plain nozzle.

Pipe the curd into a 16 cm (6¼ inch) donut ring mould. Carefully transfer to a flat tray and then into the freezer to set.

When frozen, remove the curd from the mould and return it to the freezer until needed.

CARAMEL GLAZE

150 ml (5 fl oz) pure (pouring) cream (35% fat)

¼ vanilla bean, split and seeds scraped

190 g (6¾ oz) caster (superfine) sugar

1½ tablespoons cornflour (cornstarch)

35 g (1¼ oz) white chocolate, chopped or buttons

2½ sheets titanium-strength gelatine, softened in cold water

Put the cream and vanilla bean and seeds into a saucepan and bring to the boil.

Meanwhile, put 175 g (6 oz) of the sugar in a saucepan with 140 ml (4¾ fl oz) of water over medium heat, stirring until the sugar just dissolves. Use a thermometer to measure when the mixture reaches 204°C (405°F) and turns caramel in colour. Whisking constantly, pour the boiled cream over the caramel.

Combine the remaining caster sugar and cornflour in a bowl and add 1 tablespoon of water, stirring to make a paste. Add the paste to the caramel mixture.

Bring the caramel mixture back to the boil and continue cooking, whisking constantly, for a few more minutes, until thickened.

Put the white chocolate in a heatproof bowl, pour the caramel mixture over and stir until the chocolate is melted and the mixture is smooth. Add the softened gelatine and stir until dissolved.

Strain into a jug and cover the surface with plastic wrap. Set aside until ready to glaze the dessert.

MILK CHOCOLATE MOUSSE

60 ml (2 fl oz/¼ cup) pure (pouring) cream (35% fat), plus 150 ml (5 fl oz) extra

60 ml (2 fl oz/¼ cup) milk

1 large egg yolk

2 tablespoons caster (superfine) sugar

1 sheet titanium-strength gelatine, softened in cold water

200 g (7 oz) milk chocolate, chopped or buttons

Bring the milk and cream to the boil in a medium saucepan over medium heat.

Meanwhile, whisk together the egg yolks and sugar. Pour a small amount of the boiling milk

mixture into the egg yolk mixture. Whisk together, then pour back into the saucepan.

Continue to stir with a spatula until the mixture reaches 85°C (185°F) or until it coats the back of a spoon. This will form an anglaise (see glossary). Remove from the heat and stir in the softened gelatine, squeezed gently to remove excess water.

Put the chocolate in a heatproof bowl and pour the anglaise over, whisking until smooth and fully combined. Set aside to cool to 30°C (86°F).

Meanwhile, whisk the extra cream to soft peaks and fold into the cooled anglaise. Transfer the mousse to a piping (icing) bag fitted with a size 13–15 plain nozzle.

TO ASSEMBLE

Set an 18 cm (7 inch) donut ring mould on a flat tray and fill the mould halfway with the chocolate mousse.

Remove the passionfruit curd ring from the freezer and set it into the mould on the top of the mousse, making sure the curd is level with the top of the mousse.

Pipe in a layer of mousse on top of the curd until the mould is three-quarters full, then place the banana bread ring with the chocolate crunch side down. Press down so that the banana bread is level with the top of the mould.

Use a palette knife to level off the mousse and then transfer to the freezer until frozen.

WHITE CHOCOLATE SPATTER

50 g (1¾ oz) cocoa butter

2 teaspoons titanium white food colouring powder

Put the cocoa butter in a microwave-proof bowl and heat in 40-second bursts, stirring between each burst, until completely melted.

Stir in the titanium food colouring powder and blend until combined. Strain through a fine sieve into a small bowl. Cool the mixture to 34°C (93°F) or just below body temperature.

CONTINUED >>

They say that **the way to anyone's heart** is through food, so when I wanted to **be romantic**, I created a cake with **all the flavours Casey loves.**

PASSION-ATE ABOUT CASEY PAGE 132

SALTED CARAMEL GANACHE

80 g (2¾ oz) caster (superfine) sugar
110 ml (3¾ fl oz) pure (pouring) cream (35% fat)
150 g (5½ oz) white chocolate, chopped or buttons
sea salt

Heat a medium saucepan over high heat and then reduce the heat to medium. Carefully put a third of the sugar into the hot saucepan and make a dry caramel. Continue adding the sugar until all is incorporated and a golden brown colour is achieved.

Meanwhile, bring the cream to the boil in a small saucepan. When the caramel has become golden brown, remove it from the heat and carefully pour in the boiling cream, stirring until all of the caramel has dissolved.

Put the white chocolate in a heatproof bowl and pour the caramel liquid over, stirring until completely combined. Blend with a handheld blender until the ganache is shiny. Lay a piece of freezer film on the surface and set aside in a cool area for 24 hours, ideally.

––––––––––

SALTED CARAMEL MACARONS

125 g (4½ oz/1¼ cups) almond meal
125 g (4½ oz/1 cup) icing (confectioners') sugar
3 egg whites, at room temperature, divided in half
125 g (4½ oz) caster (superfine) sugar
brown food colouring
50 g (1¾ oz) pailleté fuilletine (see glossary)

Preheat the oven to 120°C (248°F). Line 2 baking trays with baking paper and set aside.

Sift the almond meal and icing sugar together and set aside in a bowl with half the egg whites.

Put the remaining egg whites into the bowl of an electric mixer fitted with the whisk attachment.

Combine the sugar with 2 tablespoons of water in a saucepan and heat to 121°C (250°F). When the mixture reaches 115°C (239°F), turn on the electric mixer and start to whisk the egg whites. Slowly add the hot syrup and whisk until just warm. Add the brown food colouring.

Mix the almond meal, icing sugar and egg whites into a paste. Fold the meringue into the paste and stir until combined. Continue stirring, or massaging, the mixture, making sure to scrape the bottom of the bowl. The mixture needs to be of a dropping consistency.

Transfer the mixture to a piping (icing) bag with a large plain nozzle and pipe 50 round dollops onto the baking trays. Tap the trays to encourage the mixture to level itself out.

Set aside for 45–60 minutes, until the macarons have formed a skin. Bake for 12 minutes, then turn the trays and bake for a further 12 minutes until crisp.

Cool on the tray. Put the salted caramel ganache in a piping (icing) bag and pipe the ganache onto the flat side of half the macarons. Top each one with the remaining macarons. Store in an airtight container for up to 1 week.

––––––––––

MANGO COULIS

50 ml (1¾ fl oz) mango purée (see glossary)
25 g (1 oz/¼ cup) pure icing (confectioners')
    sugar, sifted

In a small saucepan, bring the mango purée just to the boil over medium heat. Make sure not to let it boil, or it will lose the fresh flavour.

Remove from the heat and whisk in the icing sugar. Return to medium heat. Whisk constantly until the icing sugar has completely dissolved.

Remove the pan from the heat and carefully pour the coulis into a small stainless steel bowl. Cover the surface with plastic wrap and cool in the refrigerator.

Fill 8 pipettes (see glossary) with the coulis and set aside in the refrigerator until needed for garnishing.

––––––––––

WHITE CHOCOLATE DECORATIONS

150 g (5½ oz) white chocolate (28% cocoa butter), tempered (see page 232)
2 teaspoons titanium white colour powder

Line a 20 x 30 cm (8 x 12 inch) tray with an acetate sheet and reserve until needed.

Pour the tempered chocolate onto the tray and use a palette knife to spread it out evenly and thin. Cool until firm but not hard.

Cut out shapes: three 4 cm (1½ inch) circles, three 4 x 2 cm (1½ x ¾ inch) rectangles, three 3 cm (1¼ inch) squares and three 4 cm (1½ inch) triangles.

Lay a piece of baking paper on top and then place another flat tray on top and transfer to the refrigerator to set completely.

––––––––––

CARAMEL POPCORN

40 g (1½ oz) popcorn kernels
vegetable oil, for popping
110 g (3¾ oz/½ cup) caster (superfine) sugar
40 g (1½ oz) unsalted butter, at room temperature
10 g (⅜ oz) trimoline (see glossary)

Put the popcorn kernels in a medium saucepan with just enough vegetable oil to lightly coat the kernels. Cover the saucepan with foil and set over medium heat.

When the popping starts, shake the saucepan constantly until the popping stops. Transfer popcorn to a bowl and cover with foil to keep warm.

Line a large baking tray with baking paper and spray with baking spray. Set aside. In a large saucepan, combine the sugar, butter and trimoline and stir. Clean down the side of the saucepan with water and a pastry brush.

Set the saucepan over high heat and bring the mixture to a golden caramel colour.

Remove from the heat and add the warm popcorn. Quickly stir the caramel around the popcorn to ensure an even coverage.

Carefully pour the popcorn out onto the prepared tray and spread out. Cool slightly and then pull the popcorn into small clumps. Allow to cool completely and store in an airtight container until needed.

––––––––––

TO PLATE

Cut the loaf of banana bread into small cubes.

Reheat the caramel glaze to 40°C (104°F) and the white chocolate graffiti mixture to 34°C (93°F).

Remove the cake from the freezer and set on a wire rack over a tray to catch drips. Pour over the warmed glaze until the cake is completely covered.

Using a clean dry pastry brush, spatter the chocolate graffiti mixture on one side of the cake.

Carefully transfer the cake to a presentation platter and decorate the non-graffiti side with the salted caramel macarons, white chocolate shapes, caramel popcorn, banana bread cubes and mango coulis pipettes.

––––––––––

ROCKSTAR TWIST

I can't give any better tips than to make all of the elements in stages and have them all ready when you start to assemble the desserts in this chapter. Use a sugar thermometer to ensure that the glaze and chocolate graffiti mixture are at the correct temperature.

I made this dessert for the first time for a dessert degustation: 22 people and five courses. I piped my meringue upside down and quenelled my sorbet on top. It blew everyone away on the night, along with my social media followers.

Note: You will need eight 150–200 ml (5–7 fl oz) glasses to serve this dish.

SERVES 8

VANILLA SABLE

350 g (12 oz) unsalted butter, at room temperature
180 g (6¼ oz/1½ cups) pure icing (confectioners') sugar, sifted
1 egg
1 vanilla bean, split and seeds scraped
500 g (1 lb 2 oz/2⅓ cups) plain (all-purpose) flour, sifted

In an electric mixer fitted with the paddle attachment, beat the butter and icing sugar on medium speed until light and fluffy.

Reduce the speed to low. Add the egg and the vanilla seeds. Return to medium speed and beat until well combined. Reduce the speed to low again and add the flour in 2 batches. When all of the flour has been added, beat until a smooth dough is formed.

On a very lightly floured surface, shape the dough into flat rectangles. Wrap in plastic wrap and chill for at least 1 hour in the refrigerator. This recipe is about double the amount you will need, so freeze half the dough for another batch, or bake double the amount of sable discs and store them in an airtight container for up to 2 weeks.

Preheat the oven to 170°C (325°F) and line a baking tray with baking paper.

Take the dough out of the refrigerator. On a lightly floured surface, roll out the dough to 1 cm (⅜ inch) thick. Cut out 8 discs just a little larger than the top diameter of the serving glasses. Place the discs 3 cm (1¼ inches) apart on the baking tray.

Lay another piece of baking paper on top and then a flat tray or 2 silicone mats, to keep the sable flat.

Bake for about 8 minutes, then turn the trays around in the oven and bake for another 7 minutes or until golden brown. Remove from the oven and allow to cool on the tray. Reserve in an airtight container until needed.

PASSIONFRUIT POSSET

500 ml (17 fl oz/2 cups) pure (pouring) cream (35% fat)
400 g (14 oz) caster (superfine) sugar
125 ml (4½ fl oz/½ cup) passionfruit purée (see glossary)

Set the serving glasses on a tray.

Put the cream and sugar in a medium to large saucepan over high heat and bring to the boil. Boil for 4 minutes, then turn off the heat and whisk in the passionfruit purée.

Return to the heat and boil for another 4 minutes.

Remove from the heat and pour 100 ml (3½ fl oz) into each of the serving glasses. Carefully put the tray with the glasses into the refrigerator to set for 30–60 minutes.

MANGO AND PASSIONFRUIT JELLY

200 ml (7 fl oz) passionfruit purée (see glossary)
140 ml (4¾ fl oz) mango purée (see glossary)
1 tablespoon caster (superfine) sugar
1 sheet titanium-strength gelatine, softened in cold water

Put the fruit purées and the sugar in a small saucepan and bring just to the boil over medium heat.

Remove from the heat and stir in the softened gelatine. Strain into a plastic container through a fine sieve. Set aside to cool.

When the jelly has cooled down but not set, remove the tray of glasses from the refrigerator and pour a 5 mm (¼ inch) layer of jelly over the passionfruit posset.

Carefully return the tray to the refrigerator for the jelly layer to set.

MANGO AND PASSIONFRUIT GELATO

14 g (½ oz) sorbet stabiliser (see glossary)
350 g (12 oz) caster (superfine) sugar
70 ml (2¼ fl oz) glucose syrup (see glossary)
525 ml (18 fl oz) mango purée (see glossary)
350 ml (12 fl oz) passionfruit purée (see glossary)

Combine the stabiliser, sugar and glucose syrup in a bowl and set aside.

Using a thermometer, heat 450 ml (15½ fl oz) of water in a medium saucepan until it reaches 40°C (104°F). Remove from the heat and whisk in the sugar mixture.

Return the saucepan to the heat and use a thermometer to bring the syrup up to 65°C (149°F). Remove from the heat and strain into a bowl. Sit the bowl in a larger bowl of iced water. Chill the mixture down to 10°C (50°F).

Blend in the mango and passionfruit purées.

Churn the mixture in an ice-cream machine, following the manufacturer's instructions. Freeze until needed.

—————

TROPICAL COMPOTE

½ pineapple
1 large mango
100 g (3½ oz) mixed mango and lychee pearls
     (see glossary)
3 passionfruit

Peel and core the fresh pineapple, making sure not to take too much of the flesh off. Cut the flesh into 1 cm (⅜ inch) cubes and put them into a small bowl.

Remove the skin from the mango and cut the flesh into 1 cm (⅜ inch) cubes and add to the pineapple.

Drain syrup from the mango and lychee pearls and add them to the fruit mixture.

Cut the passionfruit in half and scrape the pulp into a separate small bowl. Stir to help break it down, make sure there are no white bits. Add to the fruit mixture and stir together. Reserve in the refrigerator until needed for assembly.

—————

ITALIAN MERINGUE

190 g (6¾ oz) caster (superfine) sugar
3 egg whites, at room temperature

Combine the sugar with 50 ml (1¾ fl oz) of water in a small saucepan and stir, brushing down the side of the saucepan with water and a pastry brush to prevent any sugar crystals forming.

Bring to the boil over high heat, stirring constantly with a wooden spoon until the sugar has dissolved. Brush down the side of the saucepan again with water and the pastry brush.

Meanwhile, put the egg whites in the bowl of an electric mixer fitted with the whisk attachment. Whisk on low speed for 3–4 minutes until soft peaks form.

Using a thermometer, bring the sugar syrup to 121°C (250°F). Increase the mixer's speed to high and pour in the hot syrup in a smooth, steady stream.

When the syrup is completely incorporated, continue to whisk for 10 minutes, until it has cooled to room temperature. At this stage the meringue will be thick, glossy and ready to use immediately.

—————

TO ASSEMBLE

1 handful of baby coriander (cilantro) sprigs

Bring the tray of glasses out of the refrigerator and spoon 1 tablespoon of the tropical compote evenly into the glasses on top of the jelly.

Put the Italian meringue into a piping (icing) bag fitted with a size 15 plain nozzle and pipe the meringue onto the vanilla sable discs. Place three sprigs of coriander on each one.

Turn the sable over so the meringue is underneath and set the sable on top of the serving glass with the meringue inside.

Quenelle a teaspoon of the sorbet on top and serve.

—————

ROCKSTAR TWIST

Small shot glasses with just the jelly and tropical compote are super-easy and fast if you don't have time to do the sorbet, meringue and the sable.

TWISTED PAGE 138

Twisted is a meringue **turned upside down**, giving it that cool edge. **Crack through the layers** to enjoy the smooth acidic textures of **the posset and sorbet.**

My chocolate cake is a 50 cm (20 inch) tall rockstar: the 'Tower of Terror' featured on *Family Food Fight* (on Australia's Channel 9). The cake had 103 steps and they even designed a special cake box to go with it. It was a talking point for the show; my social media went crazy! This is the original recipe, even more complicated than the one that featured on the show.

Note: To assemble this cake you will need round cake boards measuring 20 cm (8 inches), 15 cm (6 inches) and 10 cm (4 inches) in diameter, as well as cake dowels to support the tiers. These are available from cake decorating supply stores.

MAKES 1 CRAZY CHOCOLATE CAKE

CHOCOLATE MUD CAKE
2.97 kg (6 lb 1 oz) dark brown sugar
1.125 kg (2 lb 7 oz) dark chocolate, chopped
    or buttons
1.17 kg (2 lb 12 oz) unsalted butter
160 g (5¾ oz/1½ cups) cocoa powder
    (unsweetened), sifted
30 g (1 oz) bicarbonate of soda (baking soda)
180 g (6¼ oz) baking powder
2 kg (4 lb 8 oz) plain (all-purpose) flour
18 eggs

Preheat the oven to 165°C (320°F). You will need three 23 cm (9 inch), three 18 cm (7 inch) and two 13 cm (5 inch) round cake tins: spray them with baking spray and line with baking paper. Set the tins of the same diameter on baking trays.

In a large saucepan, combine the brown sugar, chocolate, butter, cocoa powder and bicarbonate of soda with 2.225 litres (77½ fl oz) of water. Stir and set over medium heat.

Cook until the mixture is combined and the sugar has dissolved. Stir frequently and do not allow the mixture to boil.

Remove from the heat and pour the batter into a large bowl. Whisk the mixture as it cools for 5 minutes.

Meanwhile, sift the baking powder and plain flour together. Add the flour mixture to the batter and whisk fast and hard.

Whisk the eggs in a separate bowl and add to the batter a little at a time, stirring well before adding more egg.

Weigh 1.4 kg (3 lb 2 oz) of the batter into each of the large cake tins; weigh 1 kg (2 lb 2 oz) into each of the medium tins; and weigh 500 g (1 lb 2 oz) into each of the small cake tins.

Transfer the cake tins on the trays into the oven. Bake the small tins for 40 minutes, the medium tins for 60 minutes and the large tins for 70 minutes, or until a skewer inserted into the centre comes out with some moist crumbs sticking to it, but no raw cake mixture. If your oven allows, bake all of the cakes at once and remove the trays of the smaller cakes after the allotted time has passed. Alternatively, bake the cakes in batches.

Cool the cakes completely in the tins by putting the trays in the refrigerator.

Remove the cooled cakes from the cake tins and set them on trays in the refrigerator until needed.

CHOCOLATE BISCUIT CRUNCH
25 g (1 oz) chocolate-coated malt balls
    (such as Maltesers)
25 g (1 oz) chocolate-coated, chocolate cream
    biscuits (such as Tim Tams), coarsely chopped
20 g (¾ oz) dark chocolate, chopped or buttons
1 teaspoon vegetable oil

Put the chocolate-coated malt balls into a resealable plastic bag and use a rolling pin to crush them to pieces of similar size to the chopped biscuits. Mix together in a small bowl.

In a medium microwave-proof bowl, melt the chocolate in 30-second bursts, stirring between each one, until completely melted.

Stir in the vegetable oil until smooth, then quickly fold in the crumbled pieces.

Put a 10 cm (4 inch) round mould on a tray and spread the crunch right to the edge of each insert mould. Do not press the crunch as it needs to have a rough surface.

Put the crunch into the freezer to set. Reserve until needed to assemble the cake.

PASSIONFRUIT CURD
100 ml (3½ fl oz) passionfruit purée
3 eggs, plus 1 egg yolk
140 g (5 oz) caster (superfine) sugar
1 sheet titanium-strength gelatine, softened
    in cold water
45 g (1½ oz) unsalted butter

In a medium saucepan, bring the passionfruit purée to the boil over medium heat.

Meanwhile, in a medium bowl combine the eggs, yolk and sugar. Whisk together to combine.

Carefully pour half of the boiling purée into the egg mixture and whisk well. Pour the egg mixture back into the saucepan, making sure to scrape out all the mixture, and whisk together.

Return to the stovetop over high heat and use a whisk to constantly stir the curd. Heat until the mixture reaches 80°C (176°F). Remove from the heat; the temperature will continue increasing for a short time to about 85°C (185°F). Squeeze the gelatine to get rid of the excess water and stir in the gelatine until completely dissolved.

Strain the curd through a fine sieve into a deep tray and allow to cool to 40°C (104°F). Blend in the butter using a handheld blender.

Lay two 10 cm round moulds on a flat tray and use a sauce dispenser to pour 100 g (3½ oz) of the curd into each mould. Carefully put the curd in the freezer until completely frozen. Reserve in the freezer until needed for assembly.

RASPBERRY LOLLY JELLY (gelatine) AND SYRUP
150 g (5½ oz) raspberry jelly lollies (jelly candy)
1 sheet titanium-strength gelatine, softened
    in cold water
12 fresh raspberries

Put the raspberry jelly lollies in a medium saucepan with 300 ml (10½ fl oz) of water. Stir, then heat over medium heat, until the lollies dissolve. Stir every couple of minutes, so the syrup does not catch and burn. When the lollies have completely dissolved, increase the heat to high and bring the mixture to the boil.

Remove from the heat and pour 300 ml (10½ fl oz) of the syrup into a heatproof jug and cool to room temperature. Lay plastic wrap on the surface and reserve at room temperature until ready to assemble the cake.

Meanwhile, squeeze the gelatine to get rid of the excess water and whisk into the remaining mixture, then strain into a plastic jug.

Set a 10 cm (4 inch) round mould on a flat tray and then place the raspberries in the mould. Pour 140 ml (4¾ fl oz) of the jelly mixture into the mould. Transfer to the freezer until completely frozen. Reserve in the freezer until needed to assemble the cake.

VANILLA MARSHMALLOW
40 g (1½ oz) caster (superfine) sugar
1½ sheets titanium-strength gelatine, softened
    in cold water
1 vanilla bean, seeds scraped
2 teaspoons glucose syrup

Put 50 ml (1¾ fl oz) of water in a small saucepan with the caster sugar and bring to the boil over medium heat.

Meanwhile, set a 10 cm (4 inch) round mould on a flat tray and lightly spray with baking spray.

Squeeze the gelatine to get rid of the excess water and put it in the bowl of an electric mixer fitted with the whisk attachment. Add the vanilla seeds and glucose syrup.

When the syrup starts to boil, turn the electric mixer on to medium speed and then slowly pour in the boiled syrup.

Increase the speed of the mixer to high and whisk until the marshmallow is pale and fluffy and has increased in volume, but is still warm.

Transfer the warm marshmallow into a piping (icing) bag fitted with a large plain nozzle. Pipe the marshmallow mixture into the mould. Use an offset palette knife to level off the marshmallow.

CONTINUED >>

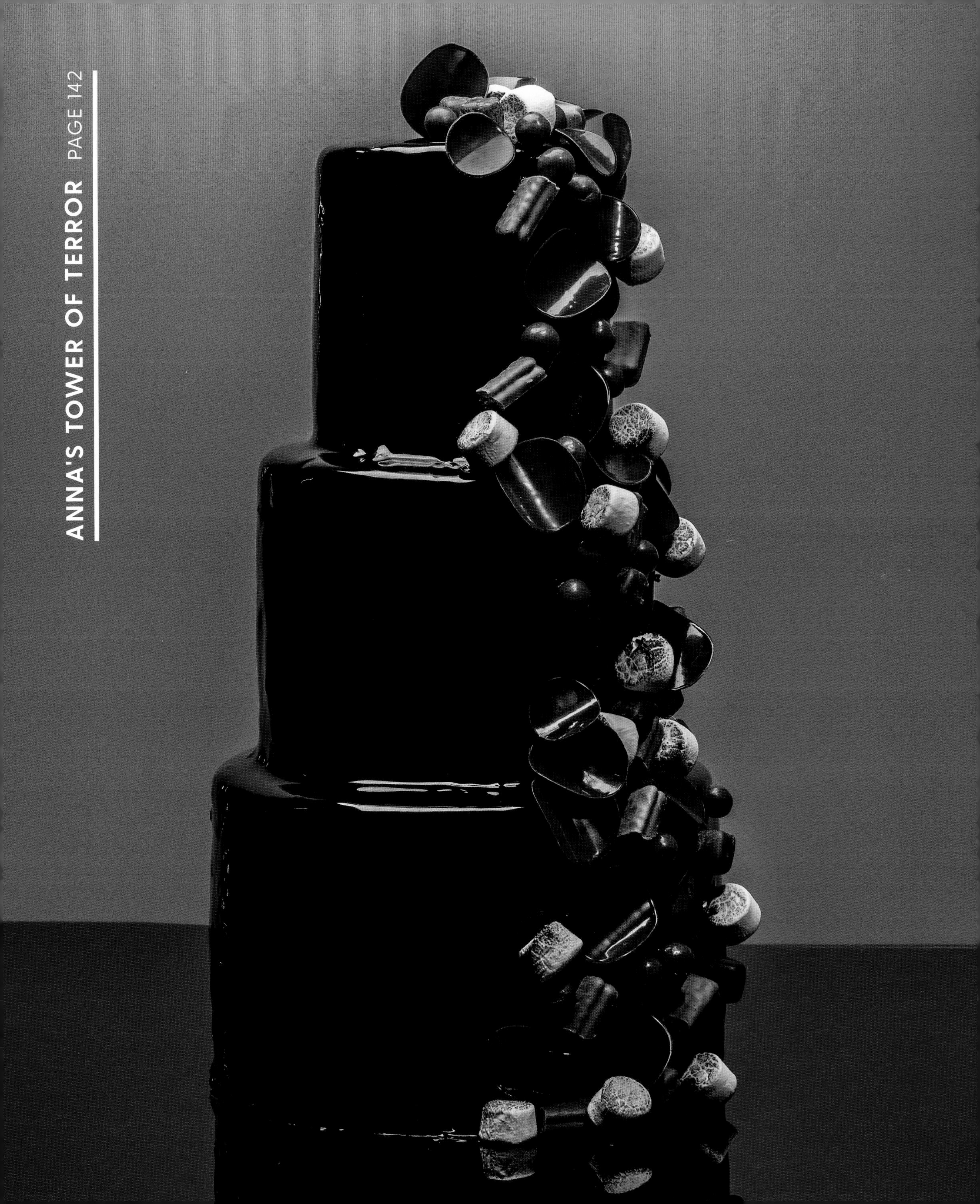

ANNA'S TOWER OF TERROR PAGE 142

Use a blowtorch to caramelise the top of the marshmallow inserts. Reserve in the freezer until needed to assemble the cake.

————

GOOEY POPCORN CARAMEL

110 g (3¾ oz) chocolate-coated chewy caramel lollies (candy), such as Fantales
55 ml (1¾ fl oz) pure (pouring) cream (35% fat)
20 g (¾ oz) caramel popcorn

In a medium saucepan, combine the chocolate-coated lollies and the cream. Cook over medium to low heat until the lollies have dissolved. Stir every couple of minutes so it does not burn.

Increase the heat to medium and bring the mixture just to the boil. Remove from the heat and pour into the bowl of an electric mixer fitted with the whisk attachment.

Whisk on high speed until the mixture has cooled and soft peaks have formed.

Meanwhile, set a 10 cm (4 inch) round mould on a flat tray and lightly spray with baking spray.

Transfer the caramel cream into a piping (icing) bag fitted with a plain nozzle and pipe 100 g (3½ oz) of caramel into the mould. Use an offset palette knife to level off the top.

Press the caramel popcorn into the caramel cream and freeze. Reserve in the freezer until ready for assembly.

————

DARK CHOCOLATE GLAZE

600 ml (21 fl oz) pure (pouring) cream (35% fat)
750 ml (26 fl oz/3 cups) glucose syrup
900 g (2 lb) caster (superfine) sugar
300 g (10½ oz) cocoa powder (unsweetened)
20 sheets titanium-strength gelatine, softened in cold water

Combine the cream, glucose and caster sugar with 245 ml (8½ fl oz) of water in a large saucepan over medium heat and bring to the boil. Remove from the heat and stir in the cocoa powder. Return to the heat and bring back to the boil, whisking until smooth.

Pour the glaze mixture into a stainless steel bowl. Using a handheld blender, blend until combined.

Squeeze the gelatine to get rid of the excess water and add it to the glaze mixture. Continue to blend until everything is incorporated.

Strain the mixture through a fine sieve and transfer to a container. Cover the surface with plastic wrap and leave in the refrigerator overnight.

————

MILO BUTTERCREAM

450 ml (15½ fl oz) milk
26 egg yolks
1.05 kg (2 lb 6 oz) caster (superfine) sugar
1. 875 kg (4 lb 2 oz) unsalted butter, at room temperature
10 egg whites
300 g (10½ oz) Nestlé MILO® (chocolate malted milk powder)

In a medium saucepan, bring the milk to the boil over high heat. Meanwhile, whisk together the egg yolks and 450 g (1 lb) of the caster sugar.

Carefully pour half of the milk onto the egg mixture and whisk well.

Pour the egg mixture back into the saucepan, making sure to scrape out all of the mixture, and whisk together. Return the saucepan to medium heat and stir constantly with a spatula until the temperature reaches 80°C (176°F).

Remove the hot anglaise from the heat and pour it into the bowl of an electric mixer fitted with the whisk attachment. Whisk the mixture until it is just warm, then gradually add the butter bit by bit. Make sure to mix each addition of the butter completely before adding more and scrape down the side of the bowl every so often. This forms a buttercream mixture.

Put the remaining caster sugar in a medium saucepan with enough water to make a slurry, and set over high heat. Clean down the sides of the pan with water and a pastry brush to prevent crystals forming.

Bring the sugar syrup to 121°C (250°F). Meanwhile, put the egg whites into the bowl of an electric mixer fitted with the whisk attachment. When the syrup reaches 115°C (239°F) start to whisk the egg whites on high speed.

When the syrup reaches 121°C, remove it from the heat and reduce the speed of the mixer. Gradually pour the syrup into the egg whites. Increase the speed to high and whisk until cool.

Remove from the mixer and add the meringue to the buttercream mixture. Whisk on medium speed until completely combined.

Put the MILO in a medium bowl and scoop 500 g (1 lb 2 oz) of the buttercream into the MILO. Whisk the MILO and buttercream until the MILO is completely dissolved. Add the MILO buttercream to the remaining buttercream and stir until completely combined.

TO ASSEMBLE THE TOP TIER

To assemble the top tier of the cake, trim the small cakes to make them 4.5 cm (1¾ inches) high. Slice the cakes horizontally into three 1.5 cm (⅝ inch) thick discs. Lay a piece of silicone paper between each disc of each cake and put them in the freezer.

Line a 13 cm (5 inch) round springform cake tin with baking paper on the bottom and acetate around the side (the acetate needs to be taped where it overlaps, to maintain the cylinder shape). On top of the baking paper, place a 10 cm (4 inch) cake board in the centre of the tin.

Begin building up the layers of the cake. Place a disc of cake in the bottom of the ring. Brush the cake with raspberry syrup. Place the disc of chocolate biscuit crunch in the centre. Fill a piping (icing) bag fitted with a size 9 nozzle with the MILO buttercream and pipe around the edge of the crunch disc, making sure not to pipe on top of the crunch.

Place another disc of cake in the tin and press down gently to make sure it is level, then brush with raspberry syrup. Place 1 disc of frozen passionfruit curd in the middle. Pipe MILO buttercream around the edge of the disc, making sure not to pipe on top of the curd.

Place another disc of cake on top of the curd and press down gently, then brush with raspberry syrup. Place the raspberry jelly disc in the centre of the cake and pipe the MILO buttercream around the edge of the disc, making sure not to pipe on top of the jelly.

Place another disc of cake in the tin and press down gently to make sure it is level, then brush with raspberry syrup. Place the remaining disc of frozen passionfruit curd in the middle. Pipe MILO buttercream around the edge of the disc, making sure not to pipe on top of the curd.

The next layer after the passionfruit curd is a disc of cake. Make sure to press down gently and brush with the raspberry syrup.

Remove the vanilla marshmallow and choc caramel popcorn discs from the moulds. Lay the torched side of the marshmallow on the smooth surface of the caramel and then use a blowtorch to toast the other side of the marshmallow disc.

Place the marshmallow and caramel insert on top of the cake layer with the marshmallow side facing down. Pipe buttercream around the edge of the disc, making sure it does not touch the disc.

Place the last disc of cake on top of the caramel and press down gently. Transfer to the freezer for 20 minutes.

TO ASSEMBLE THE BOTTOM TIERS

To assemble the bottom 2 tiers, start with the large cakes. Trim the top of the cakes so that they are 5 cm (2 inches) high and completely level.

Line a 23 cm (9 inch) round springform cake tin with baking paper on the bottom and acetate around the sides (the acetate needs to be taped where it overlaps to maintain the cylinder shape). On top of the baking paper, place a 20 cm (8 inch) cake board in the centre.

Place one of the large cakes, with the cut side facing up, and brush with raspberry syrup.

Weigh 300 g (10½ oz) of the MILO buttercream and dollop it onto the top of the cake. Use an offset spatula to spread the buttercream, starting in the middle of the cake and working evenly over the top right to the edge of the top surface.

Place down the second large cake on top, with the cut side facing down, and press down gently to make sure it sticks. Make sure it is levelled and centred. Weigh another 300 g (10½ oz) of the MILO

CONTINUED >>

buttercream and dollop it onto the top of the cake. Evenly spread out the buttercream with an offset spatula, then place the last large cake on top and press down gently to make sure it sticks. Freeze for at least 20 minutes.

Repeat for the medium cakes, using an 18 cm (7 inch) springform cake tin, a 15 cm (6 inch) cake board for the base and 200 g (7 oz) of buttercream for each layer. Freeze for at least 20 minutes.

––––––––––

TO ASSEMBLE THE TOWER

One cake at a time, remove the cake from the freezer and from the springform cake tin. Use a palette knife to spread a thin layer of buttercream over the side of the cake to form a crumb barrier.

Dollop buttercream on to the top of the cake and use an offset spatula to spread the buttercream evenly over the top of the cake and just past the edge of the cake. (Note: for the small cake, start with the sides then do the top.)

Apply more buttercream to the side of the cake, using a palette knife. Spread the buttercream out, making sure it completely covers the cake evenly.

Finally, smooth out the buttercream using a metal scraper, discarding any excess. Return each cake to the freezer for at least 20 minutes.

Bring out the large cake from the freezer and stand it on a glazing ring in a shallow tray to collect excess glaze. Insert 4 dowels at the corners of a 13 cm (5 inch) square in the centre of the cake to support the board for the cake above, cutting the dowels to the height of the cake. Place a coin-sized dollop of buttercream in the centre of the cake.

Bring out the medium cake from the freezer and set it on top of the large cake, where the cake board will be supported by the dowels. Insert four dowels at the corners of a 7.5 cm (3 inch) square in the centre of the cake to support the board for the cake above, cutting the dowels to the height of the cake. Place a coin-sized dollop of buttercream in the centre of the cake.

Bring out the small cake from the freezer and set it on top of the medium cake, gently pressing it down to make sure it is level.

Melt the chocolate glaze in a microwave to 33°C (91°F) then use a handheld blender to blend the glaze until smooth; try not to get any bubbles. Transfer the glaze to a jug for easy pouring.

Pour the glaze straight onto the centre of the top cake, working quickly for even coverage. Use an offset palette knife to smooth the top of the small cake and remove excess glaze (this is to be done immediately to prevent run lines in the glaze). Leave for 1 minute for the glaze to drip off. Use the palette knife to remove drips at the base of the cake as well.

Very carefully transfer the glazed cake to the serving plate and then decorate.

––––––––––

DECORATIONS

30 tempered chocolate discs, curled (see page 232)
4 chocolate-filled chocolate-coated biscuits (such as Tim Tams), quartered
16 marshmallows, toasted
30 chocolate-coated malt balls (such as Maltesers)
12 chocolate-coated chewy caramels (such as Fantales)

Decorations pictured include tempered chocolate discs, chocolate-coated malt balls, chocolate-coated biscuits and toasted marshmallows and chocolate-coated caramels, but you can use any of your favourite ready-made sweet treats.

Stick the chocolate decorations to the glaze. Use toothpicks to secure the marshmallows.

––––––––––

ROCKSTAR TWIST

This is seriously a monster of a task, so do it in stages — even over a few days is just fine. I tend to do it over a week, but do a lot of them. Make sure that all of the cake layers are even, the temperatures are correct and the presentation is perfect.

My 2017 *MasterChef Australia* creation, the Firecracker, went off with a bang. My Firecracker popped once I lit it up: inside, it is fun and cool, with caramel popcorn, marshmallow, pop rocks, roasted milk chocolate and more. Tasty, and made to share.

MAKES 1 BANGING DESSERT

ROASTED MILK CHOCOLATE

300 g (10½ oz) Alunga milk chocolate (41%), chopped or buttons
2 teaspoons skim milk powder
1 vanilla bean, split and seeds scraped

Preheat the oven to 120°C (250°F). Lay a silicone mat on a baking tray. Spread the chocolate, skim milk powder and the vanilla bean and seeds onto the mat and stir until well combined.

Roast for 10 minutes or until the chocolate has completely melted.

Use a large offset palette knife to spread the chocolate evenly, bringing the chocolate from the sides into the middle of the tray to incorporate the mixture, then spread the melted chocolate out again to form a completely smooth and even layer.

Return the tray to the oven for 10 minutes at a time, taking the tray out and spreading out the chocolate evenly as before. Repeat another three times or until the chocolate has a roasted smell, is darker in colour and all the skim milk powder has dissolved.

Remove from the oven and continue spreading the chocolate until it cools and starts to become smooth and shiny. Discard the vanilla bean.

Cool at room temperature and reserve until ready to make the chocolate mousse.

PEANUT GRUE DISCS

40 g (1½ oz) blanched unsalted peanuts
40 g (1½ oz) cacao nibs (see glossary)
80 g (2¾ oz) caster (superfine) sugar
1 large pinch yellow pectin (see glossary)
25 ml (1 fl oz) milk
25 ml (1 fl oz) glucose syrup
65 g (2½ oz) unsalted butter, at room temperature
1 teaspoon powdered cocoa butter
sea salt

Preheat the oven to 170°C (325°F). Lay a silicone mat on a baking tray.

Put the peanuts into the bowl of a food processor. Blitz until the peanuts are an even crumb, about the same size as the cacao nibs. Transfer the peanuts to a small bowl, add the cacao nibs and set aside until required.

Combine the sugar and pectin in a small bowl and stir, then set aside. Put the milk and glucose syrup in a small copper saucepan and bring just to boiling point. Add the butter and stir until the butter has melted. Remove from the heat.

Use a small whisk to mix the sugar and pectin into the milk mixture. Return to the heat and use a thermometer to measure when the mixture has reached 106°C (223°F), then remove from the heat.

Pour the mixture into the bowl of cacao nibs and peanuts. Add a pinch of sea salt and stir until the mixture becomes a thick paste.

Lay a sheet of baking paper on a clean work surface. Pour the grue mixture into the middle of the sheet of baking paper. Cover with a second sheet of baking paper. Use a rolling pin to roll the grue mixture out to 2 mm (¹⁄₁₆ inch) thick, between the two sheets of baking paper. Transfer the paper and grue to a large flat tray and freeze for at least 20 minutes.

Peel away the top sheet of baking paper and carefully turn the grue onto the silicone mat on the baking tray. Peel away the baking paper backing and bake for 10–12 minutes, until golden brown.

While the grue is still hot, sift the powdered cocoa butter over it in an even layer. Allow to cool slightly, then use a circle cutter to cut out four 3.5 cm (1⅜ inch) discs. Leave the discs on the tray to cool and set aside at room temperature until needed to assemble the firecracker.

RASPBERRY MARSHMALLOW

100 ml (3½ fl oz) raspberry purée (see glossary)
80 g (2¾ oz) caster (superfine) sugar
1 tablespoon glucose syrup (see glossary)
3 sheets titanium-strength gelatine, softened
    in cold water

Lay a silicone sheet of 3 cm (1¼ inch) round disc moulds on a baking tray and set aside.

Combine the raspberry purée, sugar and glucose in a small saucepan and bring to the boil, stirring occasionally

When the purée mixture starts to boil, remove it from the heat. Squeeze out the softened gelatine to remove excess water and add to the mixture. Stir until the gelatine has completely dissolved.

Pour the syrup into the bowl of an electric mixer fitted with the whisk attachment. With the mixer on high speed, whisk for 6–8 minutes until the marshmallow is pale and fluffy and has increased in volume, but is still warm.

Transfer the warm mixture to a piping (icing) bag fitted with a plain nozzle. Pipe the marshmallow mixture into four of the disc moulds, filling them to the top. Use a small, offset palette knife to level off the marshmallow and freeze.

———————

RASPBERRY COLD-SET BRULÉE

25 g (1 oz) caster (superfine) sugar
3 eggs
50 ml (1¾ fl oz) pure (pouring) cream (35% fat)
155 ml (5 fl oz) raspberry purée (see glossary)
¾ sheet titanium-strength gelatine, softened
    in cold water

Lay a silicone sheet of 3 cm (1¼ inch) round disc moulds on a baking tray and set aside. Alternatively, you can use the empty moulds in the sheet containing the marshmallow (see above).

Whisk the sugar and eggs together in a medium bowl and set aside until required.

Combine the cream and raspberry purée in a small saucepan over medium heat and bring to the boil. Whisk into the reserved egg mixture. Pour the

mixture back into the saucepan and return the saucepan to the stovetop over medium heat.

Using a thermometer, gently stir the mixture with a spatula until it reaches 85°C (185°F) and thickens slightly. Remove from the heat. Squeeze out the gelatine to remove excess water and add to the mixture, stirring until it has completely dissolved.

Pass the brulée mixture through a sieve into a clean pouring jug and set aside to cool slightly.

Pour the brulée mixture into four of the disc moulds and level off the surface with a small offset palette knife. Freeze until required for assembly.

———————

PEANUT BUTTER CREMEUX

120 ml (4 fl oz) milk
120 ml (4 fl oz) pure (pouring) cream (35% fat)
100 g (3½ oz) white chocolate, chopped or buttons
80 g (2¾ oz) crunchy peanut butter
60 g (2¼ oz) caster (superfine) sugar
3 egg yolks
1 sheet titanium-strength gelatine, softened
    in cold water

Lay a silicone sheet of 3 cm (1¼ inch) round disc moulds on a baking tray and set aside. Alternatively, you can use the empty moulds in the sheet containing the marshmallow and brulée (see above).

Put the milk and cream in a small saucepan over medium heat and bring just to the boil.

Meanwhile, put the white chocolate and peanut butter into a medium heatproof bowl and set aside. Put the caster sugar and egg yolks into a separate medium bowl and whisk until well combined.

Remove the boiling milk mixture from the heat and pour half into the egg mixture, whisking well to combine. Pour the egg mixture back into the saucepan of remaining milk and cream and return to the stovetop over medium heat. Continue to cook, stirring constantly, until the anglaise mixture reaches 65°C (149°F). Remove from the heat.

Squeeze the gelatine to remove excess water and add to the anglaise, stirring well until the gelatine has dissolved completely. Strain the

CONTINUED >>

FIRECRACKER PAGE 150

anglaise through a fine sieve over the chocolate and peanut butter and whisk until combined. Transfer to a pouring jug and cool slightly.

Pour the peanut butter cremeux mixture into four of the disc moulds, filling them up to the top. Level off the mixture with an offset palette knife and freeze until required.

RASPBERRY GEL

125 ml (4 fl oz) raspberry purée
2 teaspoons lemon juice
30 g (1 oz) icing (confectioners') sugar, sifted

Lay a silicone sheet of 3 cm (1¼ inch) round disc moulds on a baking tray and set aside. Alternatively, you can use the remaining empty moulds in the sheet containing the marshmallow, brulée and cremeux (above).

Combine the raspberry purée and lemon juice in a small saucepan over medium heat and bring just to the boil.

Gradually add the sifted icing sugar to the saucepan, whisking constantly. Once the icing sugar is combined, remove from the heat and transfer to a pouring jug.

Pour the gel into the disc moulds, filling them to the top, and freeze until required for assembly.

CHOCOLATE SPONGE

5 eggs, separated, yolks lightly beaten
115 g (4 oz) caster (superfine) sugar
45 g (1½ oz) cocoa powder (unsweetened), sifted

Preheat the oven to 190°C (375°F). Spray a 16 x 23 cm (6¼ x 9 inch) baking tin with a little canola oil. Line the tin with baking paper and spray the surface again with canola oil. Set aside until needed.

Put the egg whites in the bowl of an electric mixer fitted with the whisk attachment. Whisk on high speed until soft peaks form. Gradually add the caster sugar and continue to whisk for a further 2 minutes or until the mixture is thick and glossy and all the sugar has dissolved. Rub a little of the mixture

between your fingers to check; if it's still grainy, whisk it some more.

Remove the mixture from the machine and use a silicone spatula to gently fold in the sifted cocoa powder and the egg yolks until fully incorporated, taking care not to knock too much air out of the mixture.

Pour the sponge mixture into the prepared baking tin, filling it halfway to the top. Using a small offset palette knife, level off the surface of the sponge so that it is completely even. Bake for 10–12 minutes, until a skewer inserted in the centre comes out clean.

Lift the baking paper and sponge out of the tin, transfer to a wire rack and put it in the freezer until required.

CRUNCH

100 g (3½ oz) Alunga milk chocolate (41%), chopped or buttons
2 teaspoons powdered cocoa butter
15 g (½ oz) popping candy (Pop Rocks – see glossary)
25 g (1 oz) caramel popcorn (see page 137), coarsely chopped
25 g (1 oz) sea salt–flavoured potato chips (crisps), coarsely chopped

Combine the milk chocolate and cocoa butter in a small microwave-proof bowl. Melt in 30-second bursts in the microwave, stirring between each burst, until completely melted. Cool to 30°C (86°F), then add the popping candy, caramel popcorn and potato chips and stir gently until combined. Set aside at room temperature until required.

Lay a sheet of baking paper on a clean chopping board. Remove the chilled Sponge from the freezer. Turn the sponge out onto the board, peel away the baking paper and cover with a clean sheet of baking paper. Use a rolling pin to gently roll the sponge layer to 1 cm (⅜ inch) thick.

Remove the top layer of baking paper and spread the reserved Crunch mixture evenly on top of the sponge, levelling the surface with an offset spatula. Set aside at room temperature until required.

ROASTED MILK CHOCOLATE MOUSSE

170 g (6 oz) ROASTED MILK CHOCOLATE
    (see page 150)
100 ml (3½ fl oz) milk
2 teaspoons glucose syrup (see glossary)
1 sheet titanium-strength gelatine, softened
    in cold water
200 ml (7 fl oz) pure (pouring) cream (35% fat)

Measure out the Roasted Milk Chocolate into a microwave-proof bowl. Melt in the microwave in 30-second bursts, stirring between each burst, until completely melted.

Meanwhile, put the milk and glucose syrup into a small saucepan over medium heat and bring to the boil. Remove from the heat.

Squeeze out the gelatine to remove excess water, add it to the milk mixture and whisk until the gelatine has completely dissolved.

Pour the milk mixture over the melted Roasted Milk Chocolate and whisk until completely combined. Strain through a sieve into a clean bowl and stir with a rubber spatula until the mixture has cooled to 30°C (86°F).

Meanwhile, put the cream into the bowl of an electric mixer fitted with the whisk attachment. Whisk the cream to soft peaks. When the chocolate mixture has cooled, gently fold in the cream until fully incorporated. Transfer the mousse to the refrigerator to set slightly until needed.

———

MIDDLE INSERT

On a clean work surface, lay a 30 cm (12 inch) square of plastic wrap and smooth out flat.

Remove the silicone disc mould sheet from the freezer. Push out 3 of the raspberry gel discs from the mould and stack on top of each other to form one piece, using your fingertips to smooth the seams and stick the pieces together. Lay the raspberry gel piece, lengthways, in the centre of the plastic wrap.

Lift two peanut grue discs out of the moulds and place them, flat-side inwards, on each end of the raspberry gel piece. Wrap the raspberry gel and grue piece in the plastic wrap and twist the ends to tighten and seal. Return to the freezer until required.

Lay another 30 cm (12 inch) square of plastic wrap on a clean surface and smooth out flat. Push out one of the raspberry marshmallow discs from the disc mould sheet and lay it on the plastic wrap. Then, push out one of the peanut butter cremeux discs and place it on top of the raspberry marshmallow disc. Push out one of the raspberry cold-set brulée discs and place it on top of the peanut butter cremeux.

Pick up the insert piece and use your fingertips to gently smooth the seams of the 3 layers so that they stick together to form one piece. Lay the piece down lengthways in the middle of the plastic wrap, wrap it up and twist the ends to tighten and seal.

Repeat this process with the remaining discs to make a second insert and return both inserts to the freezer until required.

Use a 4.5 cm (1¾ inch) circle cutter to cut 2 discs of sponge crunch and set aside.

———

TO ASSEMBLE THE FIRECRACKER

You will need a 16 cm (6¼ inch) length of 5 cm (2 inch) diameter PVC tube, cut in half lengthways and taped together with masking tape. Line the tube with acetate and cover one end with plastic wrap. Stand the tube on the plastic-wrapped end on a set of scales.

Gently push a metal skewer into the crunch side of one of the sponge crunch discs. Lower the disc into the tube, sponge side down, and twist the skewer to release, using a small palette knife to help push the sponge off the skewer.

Remove the roasted milk chocolate mousse from the refrigerator and whisk to remove any lumps. Transfer the mousse to a piping (icing) bag fitted with a size 9 nozzle. Carefully pipe 40 g (1½ oz) of mousse into the tube.

Remove the wrapped inserts from the freezer. Carefully remove the plastic wrap from all inserts.

Push a skewer into the raspberry marshmallow layer of one of the outer inserts and gently lower into the centre of the tube on top of the mousse. Push down gently so that the mousse moves up the sides of the tube, surrounding the insert, until it is level with the top of the insert. Twist the skewer to

CONTINUED >>

release, and use a small palette knife to push the insert off the skewer if necessary.

Pipe another 40 g (1½ oz) of mousse on top of the insert.

Take the middle insert and gently push a skewer into the peanut grue disc at one end of the insert. Carefully lower the middle insert into the tube and gently push down so that the mousse moves up the sides of the tube, surrounding the insert, until it is halfway up the side of the insert. Twist the skewer to release, and use a small palette knife to push the insert off the skewer if necessary.

Pipe another 40 g (1½ oz) of mousse on top of the insert. Gently push the skewer into the raspberry marshmallow layer of the second outer insert and lower into the tube. Push down gently so that the mousse moves up the sides of the tube, surrounding the insert, until it is level with the top of the insert. This should leave a gap of about 3 cm (1¼ inches) at the top of the tube.

Pipe a further 30 g (1 oz) of mousse on top of the raspberry marshmallow layer. Finish with the second sponge crunch disc, with the sponge upward, and push down so that the layer of sponge is surrounded by mousse and level with the top of the tube. Use a small palette knife to level off and remove any excess mousse.

Carefully transfer the tube, still upright, to a small tray and into the freezer until completely frozen.

TEMPERED CHOCOLATE SHELL

300 g (10½ oz) Cacao Barry Ocoa dark chocolate (70%), tempered (see page 232)
18 x 16.5 cm (7 x 6½ inch) and 15 x 7 cm (6 x 2¾ inch) chocolate transfer sheet (see glossary)

Remove the PVC pipe from the freezer. Gently remove the pieces of PVC tube using a small knife to cut the masking tape, taking care not to pierce the acetate or the insert. Keep the acetate around the mousse tube and return the mousse tube to the freezer until required.

Lay the transfer sheets, shiny side down, on a completely clean and cool work surface.

Pour half the tempered chocolate onto the larger rectangle of transfer sheet and use an offset palette knife to spread the chocolate very thinly and evenly, approximately 2 mm (⅛ inch) thick. Use a palette knife to lift the sheet off the bench and place it on a clean sheet of baking paper.

Repeat the method with the smaller rectangle. Set the rectangles aside to semi-set. Reserve the bowl of remaining melted chocolate for assembly.

Remove the mousse insert from the freezer and gently peel off the acetate. Lay the mousse insert along the short edge of the large rectangle of chocolate closest to you and, using the baking paper as a guide, roll the chocolate sheet around the insert, ensuring that the edge is sealed together. Place the firecracker onto a baking paper–lined tray, seam-side down, and transfer to the refrigerator to set for about 2 minutes.

Meanwhile, use a 5 cm (2 inch) circle cutter to cut two discs from the smaller rectangle, leaving the transfer sheet intact. Set aside to completely set.

TO FINISH THE FIRECRACKER

1 sparkler (handheld firework)
1 popping strip (available from party supplies stores)

When the Firecracker is set, remove from the refrigerator and carefully peel away the transfer sheet. Remove the discs from the 15 x 17 cm (6 x 6¾ inch) rectangle sheet and use a small dot of reserved melted chocolate to stick the discs to each end of the tube and encase the cracker completely.

Push the wire end of the sparkler into the top of the firecracker, then wrap the popping strip at the base of the sparkler so that when the sparkler burns down to the end it pops.

ROCKSTAR TWIST

Make sure all inserts are completely frozen. All of the inserts are to be positioned in the centre of the tube so it is centred and beautiful when you cut into it. When wrapping the firecracker, make sure that it is solid and not soft, otherwise you will struggle to wrap it.

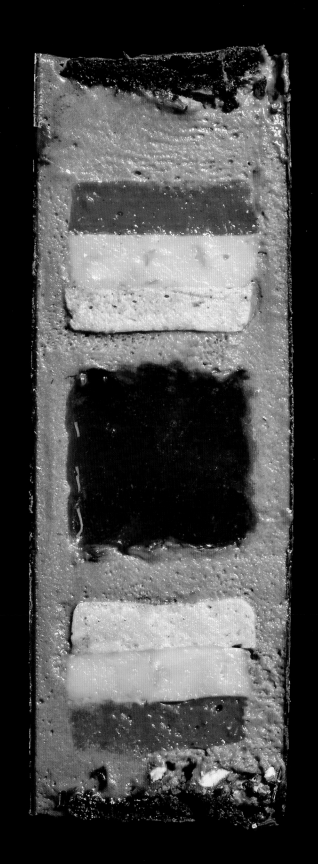

Vegan desserts are always hard to find, especially ones that taste great and look even better. This 3some offers three different chocolate desserts, from a simple petit four to a plated dessert that any fine-dining restaurant would have on the menu. There's also a version in a glass that you can serve as a canapé, dessert table or just a treat that's actually not bad for you.

I designed this to not only look amazing but taste good too; at the end of the day who wants a boring fruit plate, or even just air, when everyone else is having a wicked chocolate treat? It takes five minutes to blitz up and plate up.

SERVES 6

350 g (12 oz) silken tofu, at room temperature
200 g (7 oz) dark chocolate (70%), melted
70 ml (2¼ fl oz) soy milk
250 g (9 oz) strawberries, hulled and halved
150 g (5½ oz) raspberries
1 small handful of baby basil

Blitz the tofu in a food processor on high speed until smooth. Scrape down the side of the bowl.

Reduce the speed of the food processor and slowly pour in the melted chocolate. Return to high speed and blend until completely combined.

Reduce the speed of the food processor again and slowly pour in the soy milk, then blend until completely combined.

Line a flat tray with plastic wrap and place six 150 ml (5½ fl oz) tumblers on it. Put 4 whole raspberries into the bottom of each glass and then divide the chocolate tofu mousse evenly between the glasses. Carefully transfer the tray of glasses to the refrigerator for 10 minutes so the mousse can set.

Cut the remaining raspberries in half and combine them with the strawberries in a small bowl. Arrange the berries on top of the tofu mousse. Garnish with the baby basil leaves.

3SOME TWIST
Make sure that the tofu is at room temperature and the chocolate is fully melted, or you get chocolate chunks in the tofu. Make sure to pour it straight away, otherwise it will set due to the chocolate.

For all those with special dietary requirements, this dessert is **dairy, nut and gluten free.**

BERRY CHOC MOUSSE

This dessert is a mousse, sorbet and fruit combo. It looks so delicious that when guests see it go out at a function for those with dietary needs, suddenly everyone wants to be vegan.

SERVES 6

350 g (12 oz) silken tofu, at room temperature
200 g (7 oz) dark chocolate (70%), melted
70 ml (2¼ fl oz) soy milk
300 g (10½ oz) dark chocolate (55%), tempered (see page 232)

RASPBERRY SORBET
110 g (3¾ oz/½ cup) caster (superfine) sugar
500 ml (17 fl oz/2 cups) raspberry purée (see glossary)

TO ASSEMBLE
250 g (9 oz) strawberries, hulled and halved
150 g (5½ oz) raspberries, halved
1 small handful of baby basil

Line a baking tray with baking paper. Line six 6 cm (2¼ inch) diameter moulds with acetate or baking paper and set these on the tray.

Put the tofu in a food processor and blitz on high speed until smooth. Make sure to scrape down the side of the bowl.

Reduce the speed of the food processor and slowly pour in the melted chocolate. Return the speed to high and blend until completely combined.

Reduce the speed of the food processor again and slowly pour in the soy milk. Blend until completely combined.

Divide the mixture evenly into the rings and transfer to the freezer for at least 2 hours to set.

To make the raspberry sorbet, combine the sugar with 90 ml (3 fl oz) of water in a small saucepan over medium heat and bring just to the boil.

Put the raspberry purée into a medium bowl and, when the sugar syrup has just come to the boil, pour on top of the purée. Whisk until completely combined, then set aside to cool.

Churn the sorbet mixture in an ice-cream machine, following the manufacturer's instructions, and reserve until needed.

To make the chocolate discs, line a flat tray with an acetate sheet, then use a palette knife to spread a thin layer of the tempered chocolate onto the acetate. When the chocolate has just set, use a 6 cm (2¼ inch) round cutter to cut out 12 discs.

When the chocolate has set, lay a piece of baking paper on top of the discs and place a dry flat tray on top of that. Transfer to the refrigerator to set for a further 20–30 minutes.

Remove from the refrigerator and turn it over, so that the shiny side of the chocolate is on top. Remove the tray and the acetate sheet and reserve the discs until needed.

To assemble, lay 6 dark chocolate discs on a flat tray with the shiny side down, then unmould the tofu mousse and place one on each disc. Top the mousse with the remaining 6 discs, this time with the shiny side up.

Carefully stand each chocolate mousse sandwich on a serving plate and add the berries. When ready to serve, place a quenelle of raspberry sorbet on top of the berries and garnish with baby basil leaves.

3SOME TWIST
The chocolate tofu mousse will keep for 1–2 weeks in the freezer; don't leave it any longer than that as it tends to discolour. When you take it out of the freezer, you need to work quickly or it will soften and be hard to handle.

Petit fours can cover those with dietary needs too. For a little bit of theatre, try piping the truffle in front of your guests, tossing it in cocoa powder and serving it on a spoon.

—————

MAKES 30

—————

350 g (12 oz) silken tofu, at room temperature
200 g (7 oz) dark chocolate (70%), melted
70 ml (2¼ fl oz) soy milk
105 g (3⅝ oz/1 cup) dark chocolate cocoa powder (unsweetened)

—————

Put the tofu in a food processor and blitz on high speed until smooth. Make sure to scrape down the side of the bowl.

Reduce the speed of the food processor and slowly pour in the melted chocolate. Return the speed to high and blend until completely combined.

Reduce the speed of the food processor again and slowly pour in the soy milk. Blend until completely combined.

Put the mixture into a deep tray lined with plastic wrap and transfer to the refrigerator for 1 hour to set.

Sift the cocoa powder into a medium bowl. When the mousse is set, scoop teaspoons of the mousse into the cocoa and roll carefully between the palms of your hands to form long ovals. Make sure that the cocoa powder completely covers the mousse.

Store them in an airtight container in the refrigerator and eat within 24 hours.

—————

3SOME TWIST
The tofu is very soft to handle, so make sure it is cold. You can add dried fruit to the truffle mixture. Serving the truffles on a spoon is a great way to present it.

A melting moment of chocolate in the mouth. At **my dinner parties,** everyone has a go at **piping their own** and eating it straight away.

Can Christmas get any naughtier? These desserts are so bad, but so good at the same time. Christmas is the time to get really creative: add a fun, cool twist to traditional recipes and Santa will be sure to cross you off the naughty list this year.

Christmas in a Jar is about using whatever is lying around after Christmas lunch: the leftover Christmas cake, the fruit from the mince tarts or the cherries in the fridge.

MAKES EIGHT 250 ML (9 FL OZ/1 CUP) JARS

CHOCOLATE MOUSSE

200 g (3½ oz) caster (superfine) sugar

4 eggs, plus 2 egg yolks, extra

300 g (10½ oz) dark chocolate (63%), chopped or buttons, melted

340 ml (11¼ fl oz) pure (pouring) cream (35% fat), lightly whipped

In a small saucepan, combine the sugar with 50 ml (1¾ fl oz) of water and stir together. Clean down the side of the saucepan with water and a pastry brush to prevent crystals forming. Over high heat, use a sugar thermometer to measure when the temperature reaches 121°C (250°F).

Meanwhile, put the eggs and yolks into the bowl of an electric mixer fitted with the whisk attachment. Whisk on high speed until light and pale.

Remove the sugar syrup from the heat and reduce the speed of the mixer to medium. Slowly pour the sugar syrup into the bowl.

Return the mixer to high speed and continue whisking until the egg yolk mixture has cooled down.

Remove from the mixer and fold in the melted chocolate by hand. Be quick, or the chocolate will set and lumps will form.

Follow the chocolate with the whipped cream, until completely combined. Cover the top with plastic wrap or freezer film and allow to set in the refrigerator for at least 1 hour or until firm.

TO ASSEMBLE

240 g (8¾ oz) Christmas cake (ready-made or leftover), crumbled, plus extra for topping

300 g (10½ oz) cherries, halved and stones removed

24 whole cherries with stems attached

Lay plastic wrap or paper towel on a flat tray and set out eight 250 ml (9 fl oz/1 cup) jars. Put 30 g (1 oz) of the Christmas cake in the bottom of each jar, pushing it to one side.

Put the chocolate mousse in a piping (icing) bag fitted with a plain nozzle and pipe the mousse into the jars, filling each one to about 3 cm (1¼ inches) from the top. Tap the jar gently to level the top.

Divide the halved cherries evenly among the jars and top with 3 whole cherries and the remaining cake crumbs.

NAUGHTY TWIST

If the mousse is too firm, beat it with the paddle attachment in an electric mixer before transferring it to the piping (icing) bag. It should be smooth and soft enough to drop evenly through the glass.

Allow people to **create their own** with all the condiments **in the middle of the table** during Christmas: they can **spice it up** and match it up **their own way.**

LOLLY-BAG HOUSE

Each Christmas my team and I build a walk-in gingerbread house in the foyer of the hotel with 1000 kg (2200 lb) of gingerbread, 500 kg (1100 lb) of lollies (candy/sweets) and 100 kg (220 lb) of icing, not to mention 200 lollipops. It gets launched with drummers, DJs and nothing but fun. Inside it's full of all the lollies that you loved as a kid. In 2017 I made a gingerbread train with wheels that moved, lights and a smoke machine.

MAKES 1 GINGERBREAD HOUSE

GINGERBREAD HOUSE DIMENSIONS
(see templates, below. Not to scale)

1 kg (2 lb 4 oz) mixed lollies (candy/sweets)

GINGERBREAD DOUGH

800 g (1 lb 12 oz) plain (all-purpose) flour
60 g (2¼ oz) baking powder
1 teaspoon ground ginger
3 teaspoons ground mixed spice
1 teaspoon salt
100 g (3½ oz) unsalted butter, at room temperature
200 ml (7 fl oz) honey
180 g (6¼ oz) brown sugar
zest of 2 lemons
4 eggs
125 ml (4 fl oz/½ cup) milk

ROYAL ICING

2 egg whites, at room temperature
530 g (1 lb 3 oz) pure icing (confectioners') sugar, sifted
2 teaspoons lemon juice

BACK AND FRONT WALLS
(cut two pieces)

21 cm (8¼ inches)

12 cm (4½ inches)

ROOF AND SIDE WALLS
(cut four pieces)

13 cm (5 inches)

12 cm (4½ inches)

BASE
(cut one piece)

18 cm (7 inches)

20 cm (8 inches)

Sift the flour, baking powder, spices and salt together and set aside.

In a small saucepan, melt the butter, honey and brown sugar over low heat, until the butter has melted and the sugar has dissolved. Remove from the heat and allow to cool.

Put the flour mixture and the lemon zest in the bowl of an electric mixer fitted with the paddle attachment. Beat on low speed as you add the cooled butter mixture. Then add the eggs, one at a time, until completely incorporated.

Turn the dough out onto a lightly floured work surface and shape with your hands into a flat rectangle. Wrap in plastic wrap and chill in the refrigerator for 1–2 hours.

Preheat the oven to 160°C (315°F). Line a baking tray with baking paper.

On a flat, clean surface, roll out the chilled gingerbread dough to 1 cm (⅜ inch) thick. Cut out the required shapes, including the door and windows, using the templates as a guide. Reserve the leftover dough for GINGER NINJAS (see page 179): knead into a flat rectangle and wrap in plastic wrap, then store in the refrigerator until needed.

Lay all the gingerbread pieces on the prepared baking tray. Brush with the milk to give the gingerbread a nice gloss.

Bake for 25–30 minutes until golden brown. Remove from the oven and cool on the tray. If the gingerbread is still too soft, return it to the oven for a further 5 minutes, making sure to keep an eye out so it doesn't burn. Allow to cool and harden overnight at room temperature.

To make the royal icing, put the egg whites into the bowl of an electric mixer fitted with the paddle attachment. Beat on low speed.

Add the icing sugar, a quarter of a cup at a time, beating until completely combined before adding the next amount. Add the lemon juice and beat until combined. Cover the bowl with a damp tea towel (dish towel) to stop the icing from drying out.

Transfer the icing to a piping (icing) bag fitted with a small plain nozzle. Stand the back panel of the house in position on the base, piping the royal icing along the join on each side of the base, to secure it in place. You might need someone to help by holding the panel in position.

Next, stand one side panel at a right angle to the back panel and pipe some icing along the inside and outside base. Pipe more icing carefully down the inside of the corner join between the two panels.

Repeat with the remaining side panel and then the front panel.

Before adding the roof, fill the house with approximately 800 g (1 lb 12 oz) of mixed lollies.

To set the roof, pipe some icing along the top leading edges of the wall panels and gently place the roof pieces on top, one at a time. Pipe more icing along the top ridge of the roof and around the outside of the joins between panels. Let this set for 1–2 hours.

Using the remaining royal icing, cover the roof. Make icicles around the edges of the roof with small dollops of icing. Add lollies on the roof, then decorate the walls and around the base of the house with lollies secured by small blobs of royal icing. The house will need to dry and set for 24 hours before it can be moved.

NAUGHTY TWIST

Assemble the house in a cool, dry area. Don't rush: allow the icing to set. My favourite lollies are Allen's Party Mix, which contains things like jelly snakes (gummy snakes), jelly babies (jelly tots), raspberry jellies, strawberry and cream jellies, milk bottles and candy bananas. I also like to add freckles (chocolate nonpareils), jelly beans, licorice allsorts and Fantales (chocolate-coated chewy caramels).

Hansel and Gretel eat your heart out! **To get into the house** you just have to **smash it,** a fun family activity over **Christmas lunch.**

Christmas lunch wouldn't be the same without a trifle, especially in Australia where Christmas is a summer holiday. This is why my trifle has peaches in it, and honey ones at that.

Note: You will need a large clear glass vase or bowl, with a volume of about 5 litres (175 fl oz/20 cups).

———————

SERVES 8–10

———————

200 g (7 oz/about 20) amaretti biscuits
200 g (7 oz) caster (superfine) sugar
3 large egg whites

YELLOW PEACH JELLY
350 ml (12 fl oz) yellow peach purée (see glossary)
60 g (2¼ oz) caster (superfine) sugar
2 sheets titanium-strength gelatine, softened in
    cold water

DIPLOMAT CREAM
360 g (12¾ oz) VANILLA PASTRY CRÈME
    (see page 233)
800 g (1 lb 12 oz) pure (pouring) cream (35% fat)

ROASTED PEACHES
10 peaches
60 g (2¼ oz) unsalted butter, at room temperature
50 ml (1¾ fl oz) honey
60 g (2¼ oz) brown sugar

———————

In a small saucepan over medium heat, combine the peach purée, sugar and 300 ml (10½ fl oz) of water and bring just to the boil.

Remove from the heat, squeeze out the gelatine to get rid of excess water and add to the purée mixture. Stir until dissolved.

Strain into the vase or bowl and lay plastic wrap on the surface of the jelly. Cool to 30°C (86°F).

Line a flat tray with plastic wrap to prevent slipping and place the vase or bowl on the tray. Pour the cooled jelly into the container and carefully transfer to the refrigerator for 2–3 hours to set.

To make the Diplomat Cream, put the Vanilla Pastry Crème into the bowl of an electric mixer fitted with the whisk attachment and whisk on medium to high speed until smooth.

Reduce the speed to low and slowly pour in the cream. Once all the cream is added, increase the speed to medium and whisk to semifirm peaks. Reserve in the refrigerator until ready to assemble the trifle.

To roast the peaches, preheat the oven to 190°C (375°F). Spray a baking tray with baking spray.

Cut the peaches in half and discard the seed. Put the peach halves onto the prepared baking tray, cut-side down.

On top of each peach place a teaspoon of unsalted butter, then sprinkle with the brown sugar and drizzle with the honey.

Bake for 10 minutes or until tender and the skin on the peaches pulls away. Remove from the oven and cool on the tray until cool enough to handle. Carefully pull away the skin and reserve the peaches until needed.

To assemble the trifle, remove the container with the jelly from the refrigerator and arrange half of the roasted peach cheeks on top of the jelly.

Spoon a third of the Diplomat Cream on top of the roasted peaches and spread out level.

Top the first layer of cream with the amaretti biscuits. Evenly spread another third of the cream on top of the biscuits.

Arrange the remaining roasted peaches on the cream and then spread the rest of the diplomat cream on top. Return to the refrigerator for 30 minutes to set.

Meanwhile, combine the caster sugar in a small saucepan with enough water to make a slurry and cook over high heat. Bring the sugar syrup to 121°C (250°F), using a sugar thermometer to measure.

Put the egg whites into the bowl of an electric mixer fitted with the whisk attachment, and when the syrup has reached 118°C (244°F), start to whisk on high speed.

Reduce the speed to low and slowly pour the syrup into the egg whites. Return to high speed and whisk until cold to make an Italian meringue.

Retrieve the assembled trifle from the refrigerator and dollop the meringue on top, creating lots of spiky peaks. Use a blowtorch to lightly caramelise the meringue.

NAUGHTY TWIST

For even faster assembly, you can always replace the roasted peaches with tinned peaches; just make sure to drain the syrup or the trifle will be wet and runny. If you don't have time to make the diplomat cream, use cream whipped with a little vanilla and icing (confectioners') sugar.

This is very much a **cheat's Christmas trifle:** the amaretti biscuits are purchased ready made for **quick and easy assembly.**

HONEY I'M CHEATING WITH PEACHES   PAGE 174

I don't go traditional with plain gingerbread men, I go the whole ninja. They're super-cool and loads of fun to decorate, as well.

MAKES 15

Gingerbread dough (see page 170: use the scraps leftover from the GINGERBREAD HOUSE)
100 ml (3½ fl oz) milk
1 quantity ROYAL ICING (see page 170)
Food colouring liquid in several colours

Preheat the oven to 160°C (315°F). Line a baking tray with baking paper.

On a lightly floured work surface, roll out the gingerbread dough to 5 mm (¼ inch) thick. Cut out all the ginger ninjas, lay them on the baking tray (leave gaps between them to allow for spreading) and brush with the milk.

Bake the ninjas for 20–30 minutes until golden brown, then cool on the tray.

Prepare the royal icing, then divide it into smaller bowls. Cover the bowls with a damp cloth when not working with the icing.

Add food colouring powder to each bowl, a little at a time. Mix well, adding more liquid to make a stronger colour.

To make a paper piping (icing) bag, cut a large triangle of baking paper. While holding on to one corner of the baking paper, bring the other corner up and across to form a cone. Fold the ends over at the open end of the cone and secure with masking tape or a staple.

Make a piping bag for each icing colour and fill each bag. Decorate the Ginger Ninjas as desired.

NAUGHTY TWIST
You can buy ninja-shaped cutters from cake decorating supply stores or draw your own designs on baking paper and transfer them to the gingerbread. Cut them out with a small sharp knife. It's important not to let the icing dry out before piping the decorations, so have damp cloths or paper towel on hand to keep it moist until you need it. If you don't want to make your own paper piping bags, you can use an ordinary one fitted with a fine nozzle.

I've always been told not to **play with my food**, but when you have freshly baked **ginger ninjas** it's irresistible... **karate chop!** Bite off an arm or a leg **or even the head.**

SANTA'S HAT

I use these Santa's hats for afternoon tea over the Christmas period; I make them larger to serve as petite cakes and then I make even bigger ones for the buffet.

MAKES 30

VANILLA MARSHMALLOW

160 g (5¾ oz) caster (superfine) sugar
2 vanilla beans, seeds scraped
6 sheets titanium-strength gelatine, softened in
    cold water
2 tablespoons glucose syrup
200 g (7 oz) desiccated (finely shredded) coconut

Combine 100 ml (3½ fl oz) of water in a small saucepan with the caster sugar and vanilla seeds and bring to the boil.

Meanwhile, squeeze excess water out of the gelatine and put it with the glucose syrup in the bowl of an electric mixer fitted with the whisk attachment.

When the syrup starts to boil, whisk the gelatine on medium and slowly add the boiling syrup.

Increase the speed to high and whisk the marshmallow until warm.

Meanwhile, fit a piping (icing) bag with a size 7 plain nozzle and line a baking tray with acetate. Spray the acetate with baking spray.

When the marshmallow is just warm, stop the mixer and half-fill the piping bag with the mixture.

Pipe the marshmallow in a straight line onto the sprayed acetate. Once all the marshmallow has been piped on, sprinkle coconut on top. Spray another piece of acetate and place it on top of the marshmallow with the sprayed side down and leave them to set overnight.

RED GLAZE

680 g (1 lb 8 oz) white chocolate (28%),
    chopped or buttons
250 ml (9 fl oz/1 cup) milk
80 ml (2½ fl oz/⅓ cup) glucose syrup (see glossary)
1½ sheets titanium-strength gelatine, softened in
    cold water
½ teaspoon Intense Red food colouring powder

Put the white chocolate in a heatproof bowl. Bring the milk and glucose to the boil in a small saucepan.

Squeeze out excess water from the gelatine and add to the boiling milk mixture with the red food colouring, stirring until both have dissolved. Strain over the chocolate through a fine sieve.

Using a handheld blender, blend the glaze until smooth. Make sure to put the end of the hand blender on its side, to reduce air bubbles.

Transfer the glaze to a plastic container and cover the surface with plastic wrap, then put it into the refrigerator overnight.

VANILLA SABLE

90 g (3¼ oz) unsalted butter, at room temperature
45 g (1½ oz) pure icing (confectioners') sugar, sifted
½ egg
½ vanilla bean, seeds scraped
125 g (4½ oz) plain (all-purpose) flour, sifted, plus
    extra for rolling the dough

In the bowl of an electric mixer fitted with the paddle attachment, beat the butter and icing sugar on medium speed until light and fluffy.

Reduce the speed to low and add the egg and vanilla seeds, then continue mixing until all combined.

Add the sifted flour in 2 batches. Continue to beat until a smooth dough has formed.

Turn the dough onto a lightly floured surface and shape it into square shape. Wrap it in plastic wrap and chill for at least 30 minutes in the refrigerator.

Preheat the oven to 170°C (325°F) and line a baking tray with baking paper.

Remove the dough from the refrigerator and bring it to room temperature. On a lightly floured work surface, roll out the dough to 1 cm (⅜ inch) thick. Cut out thirty 5 cm (2 inch) discs and place them 3 cm (1¼ inches) apart on the prepared baking tray. Cover with another piece of baking paper on top and then a flat tray, to keep the sable flat.

Bake for about 11 minutes, then turn the trays around in the oven and bake for another 11 minutes or until golden brown. Transfer the sables to a wire rack to cool. Reserve in an airtight container until needed.

VANILLA COLD-SET BRULÉE

200 ml (7 fl oz) pure (pouring) cream (35% fat)
1 vanilla bean, split and seeds scraped
25 g (1 oz) caster (superfine) sugar
1 egg, plus 2 egg yolks, extra
1½ sheets titanium-strength gelatine, softened
    in cold water

Bring the cream and vanilla bean with the seeds to the boil in a small saucepan over medium heat.

Meanwhile, whisk the sugar, eggs and egg yolks together in a small heatproof bowl, until just combined.

Pour half of the boiling liquid into the egg mixture and whisk to combine. Pour the egg mixture back into the saucepan and return to low heat.

Use a spatula or wooden spoon to stir the mixture gently until it reaches 85°C (185°F) or until it thickens and coats the back of a spoon. Remove from the heat. Squeeze the excess water out of the gelatine and stir it into the mixture. Strain through a fine sieve into a medium bowl. Cover the surface with plastic wrap and chill in the refrigerator to 40°C (104°F) or just above body temperature.

Set a sheet of 3.5 cm (1⅜ inch) sphere moulds on a flat tray that will fit into the freezer. Pour the chilled mixture into the moulds. Carefully place the tray in the freezer, making sure it is perfectly level, until ready for assembly.

––––––––––

BERRY MOUSSE

160 ml (5¼ fl oz/⅔ cup) raspberry purée (see glossary)
160 ml (5¼ fl oz/⅔ cup) strawberry purée (see glossary)
2 sheets titanium-strength gelatine, softened
    in cold water
160 g (5¾ oz) white chocolate (28%), chopped
    or buttons
340 ml (11½ fl oz) pure (pouring) cream (35% fat),
    lightly whipped

Combine the raspberry and strawberry purée in a small saucepan and bring to the boil. Squeeze the gelatine to remove excess water and stir it into the purée mixture until completely combined. Set aside.

Put the white chocolate into a medium heatproof bowl and strain the purées over the chocolate using a fine sieve.

Stir, making sure all the chocolate has melted. Cover the surface with plastic wrap and allow to cool to 40°C (104°F).

Fold in the whipped cream.

Set a sheet of 4.5 cm (1¾ inch) sphere moulds on a flat tray. Transfer the berry mousse to a piping (icing) bag fitted with a plain nozzle.

Pipe the berry mousse halfway up the side of each mould. Remove the brulée moulds from the freezer and carefully insert each brulée dome into one of the moulds with the berry mousse. Push down gently so that the mousse comes up the sides of the brulée. Ensure that it is level with the top of the mould and not overflowing.

Place the tray in the freezer, making sure that the tray is perfectly level, until it is time for assembly.

––––––––––

TO ASSEMBLE

Heat the glaze in a microwave to 45°C (113°F) then cool it to 35°C (95°F), slowly stirring until smooth.

Lay the vanilla sable biscuits on a flat tray, spreading them out evenly.

Remove the domes from the freezer and unmould them onto a wire rack that is standing on a tray with sides. Ensure the edges of the domes are smooth. Pour the glaze to completely cover all of the domes.

Allow excess glaze to drip off the domes and then use a palette knife to carefully transfer each dome onto a sable biscuit, making sure not to touch the glaze with your fingers.

Carefully peel the acetate off the marshmallow strips. Spray a sharp knife with baking spray and cut thirty 15 cm (6 inch) lengths.

Wrap the marshmallow strips around the base of each glazed berry mousse dome.

Cut 5 mm (¼ inch) pieces of the leftover marshmallow and carefully place one in the very centre of each dome.

––––––––––

NAUGHTY TWIST

This recipe is a good lesson in basic techniques: glaze, marshmallow, sable, mousse and brulée. With practice you can combine these elements in many different ways.

SANTA'S HAT PAGE 180

Could Santa's hat look any prettier? Small, cute and **not too naughty. Take your time** to make all the elements perfectly **to impress.**

This thick, creamy, chocolatey drink is heaven with some salted chocolate cookies. The marshmallows are ready to melt in the hot chocolate.

SERVES 6

HOT CHOCOLATE
150 g (5½ oz) drinking chocolate (sweetened cocoa)
175 g (6 oz) dark chocolate (53%), chopped or buttons
550 ml (19 fl oz) pure (pouring) cream (35% fat)
300 ml (10½ fl oz) milk

VANILLA MARSHMALLOW
80 g (2¾ oz) caster (superfine) sugar
1 vanilla bean, seeds scraped
3 sheets titanium-strength gelatine, softened in cold water
1 tablespoon glucose syrup (see glossary)
60 g (2¼ oz/½ cup) non-melting icing (confectioners') sugar (see glossary)

DOUBLE CHOCOLATE CHIP COOKIES
55 g (2 oz) unsalted butter, at room temperature
45 g (1½ oz) caster (superfine) sugar
55 g (2 oz) brown sugar
1 egg, whisked
1 teaspoon vanilla bean paste
100 g (3½ oz/⅔ cup) plain (all-purpose) flour, sifted
½ teaspoon baking powder
2 teaspoons sea salt
55 g (2 oz) dark chocolate chips (53%)
55 g (2 oz) milk chocolate chips (33.5%)

To make the marshmallow, line a 10 x 15 cm (4 x 6 inch) container with plastic wrap and spray the inside with baking spray.

Combine the sugar, vanilla seeds and 50 ml (1¾ fl oz) of water in a small saucepan. Set aside.

Squeeze the excess water out of the gelatine and put it with the glucose syrup in the bowl of an electric mixer fitted with the whisk attachment.

Put the saucepan of sugar over high heat and bring to the boil. Turn on the electric mixer to medium speed and slowly pour the boiled syrup onto the gelatine mixture.

Increase the speed to high and whisk the marshmallow for 20–25 minutes, until just warm.

Pour the marshmallow into the prepared container. Use a palette knife to spread it evenly and level. Lightly spray the top of the marshmallow with baking spray and lay plastic wrap on top. Refrigerate for 2 hours.

When ready to serve, transfer the marshmallow from the tin to a cutting board and use a knife sprayed with baking spray to cut it into 3 cm (1¼ inch) cubes. Coat each cube with non-melting icing sugar and reserve until needed.

To make the cookies, preheat the oven to 180°C (350°F) and line a baking tray with baking paper.

Put the butter, caster sugar and brown sugar in the bowl of an electric mixer fitted with the paddle attachment. Beat on medium to high speed until light and pale. Reduce the speed to low and gradually add the egg and vanilla bean paste.

Add the flour, baking powder and half the sea salt and mix until combined. Scrape down the side of the bowl making sure to scrape the bottom, and mix again. Add both types of chocolate and mix until well combined.

Roll the cookie dough into 1 tablespoon balls and flatten them slightly. Place the balls on the tray with a 3 cm (1¼ inch) gap between each one.

Sprinkle the remaining sea salt over the cookies and bake for 14–15 minutes, until golden brown. Cool on the tray and then transfer to an airtight container and reserve until needed.

To make the hot chocolate, combine the drinking chocolate and the dark chocolate in a medium heatproof bowl. Set aside.

Combine the cream and milk in a medium saucepan and bring just to the boil over high heat. Pour the hot cream mixture over the chocolate mixture and stir together until completely combined. Strain through a fine sieve. Use straight away or reserve until needed: store it in an airtight container in the refrigerator for up to 4 days.

Pour a mug of hot chocolate for Santa and serve on a plate with the cookies and marshmallows.

Not only are turntables amazing for playing tunes, they are super-cool for serving a dessert. These delicious little fruit mince tarts will be the stars of your Christmas party.

MAKES 8 TARTS

110 g (3¾ oz) icing (confectioners') sugar, for dusting the tarts

EGGNOG CHANTILLY CRÈME
280 ml (9¾ fl oz) pure (pouring) cream (35% fat)
½ vanilla bean, split and seeds scraped
½ teaspoon ground cinnamon
½ teaspoon ground nutmeg
150 g (5½ oz) white chocolate (28%), chopped or buttons

Combine the cream, vanilla bean and seeds, cinnamon and nutmeg in a small saucepan over medium heat. Bring to the boil then remove from the heat. Set aside.

Put the white chocolate into a medium heatproof bowl. Pour the hot cream mixture over the chocolate. Stir together until all the chocolate has melted.

Transfer into a container and cover the surface with plastic wrap. Store in the refrigerator overnight.

SWEET PASTE
80 g (2¾ oz) caster (superfine) sugar
80 g (2¾ oz) unsalted butter, at room temperature
150 g (5½ oz/1 cup) plain (all-purpose) flour
1 egg, beaten
¼ teaspoon vanilla bean paste

Put the caster sugar, butter and flour into the bowl of an electric mixer fitted with the paddle attachment. Beat on a medium speed until the mixture is crumbly. Reduce the speed to low and add the egg.

Add the vanilla bean paste and continue mixing on low speed until everything is incorporated.

Turn the dough onto a lightly floured work surface. Shape the dough into a flat block and wrap in plastic wrap. Rest the dough in the refrigerator for 2 hours.

Remove the sweet paste from the refrigerator 10–15 minutes before rolling. Dust the work surface with flour and roll out the dough to 3 mm (⅛ inch) thick. Cut into 6 discs, 8 cm (3¼ inches) in diameter, or big enough to cover the base and side of six 5 cm (2 inch) tart (flan) tins. Gently press the pastry into the tins. Trim any excess pastry from around the top.

Use 2.5 cm (1 inch) star cutters to cut out 12 stars from the remaining dough. Lay them on a baking tray lined with baking paper and set aside to bake along with the tarts.

FILLING

1½ tablespoons cornflour (cornstarch)

2–3 tablespoons icing (confectioners') sugar, to dust

FRUIT MINCE

4 tablespoons raisins

2 tablespoons sultanas (golden raisins)

3 tablespoons candied orange peel

3 tablespoons currants

1 apple, peeled and grated

zest and juice of 1 orange

2 teaspoons brandy

25 g (1 oz) unsalted butter, melted

1 teaspoon ground nutmeg

1 teaspoon ground ginger

95 g (3¼ oz) brown sugar

To make the fruit mince, combine all of the ingredients with 60 ml (2 fl oz/¼ cup) of water in a medium bowl. Mix it well together and set aside to marinate for 24 hours.

Preheat the oven to 180°C (350°F).

Strain the liquid from the fruit into a small saucepan and cook over low to medium heat until reduced by half.

Combine the cornflour with a splash of water to make a slurry and whisk it into the liquid. Bring to the boil, continuing to whisk until thickened.

Pour the liquid over the fruit mixture and mix it together well.

Set the tart tins with the pastry on a baking tray and put a spoonful of the fruit mince mixture into each case. Put the tarts into the oven along with the stars. Bake the stars for 10–15 minutes and the tarts for 15–20 minutes.

When the stars have cooled, dust with icing sugar.

————

TO ASSEMBLE

Use an electric mixer fitted with the whisk attachment to whisk the eggnog chantilly crème to firm peaks. Be careful not to overwhisk, or the crème will split.

Put the chantilly crème into a piping (icing) bag fitted with a V-shaped nozzle. Place a tart in the centre of the turntable and start the turntable spinning at low speed. Piping from the centre of the tart, work outwards as the tart spins on the turntable.

Repeat for the remaining tarts. Top each tart with two of the stars dusted with icing sugar.

————

NAUGHTY TWIST

Use up any leftover fruit mince by folding it through ice cream. For a party, let your guests pipe on their own chantilly crème as the turntable spins.

Fruit mince tarts are so traditional, but these have **a cool modern twist** with eggnog **chantilly crème.**

TURNTABLE TARTS PAGE 186

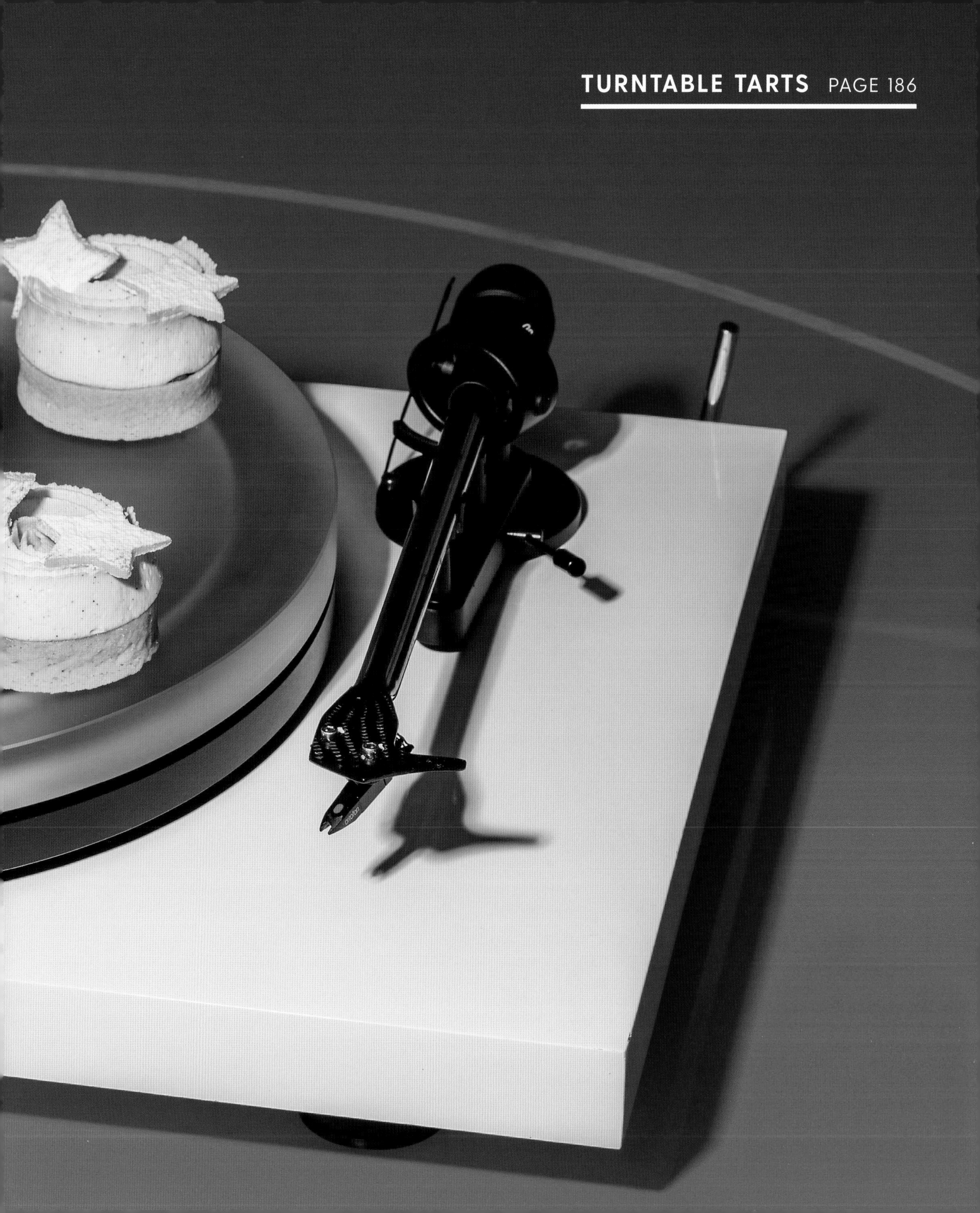

This signature dessert is traditionally round with whipped cream and fruit on top. My pavlova 3some has building blocks to share; an easy-to-construct roulade and fun ice-cream sandwiches.

When the master pâtissier Christophe Michalak came into my pastry kitchen on a promotional tour of Australia, he said the one thing he wanted to try was a pavlova. I quickly whipped up my all-time favourite recipe and sent it to his room. He requested the recipe for his book, which I bought just to see my name in it. He's a good looker and super-talented too.

SERVES 8

MERINGUE
6 egg whites, at room temperature
220 g (7¾ oz/1 cup) caster (superfine) sugar, plus extra, for sprinkling
1 teaspoon cornflour (cornstarch)
1 teaspoon vanilla bean paste

MANGO CRÈME PÂTISSIERE
100 ml (3½ fl oz) mango purée (see glossary)
100 ml (3½ fl oz) milk
½ vanilla bean, split and seeds scraped
3 egg yolks
1 tablespoon custard powder
50 g (1¾ oz) caster (superfine) sugar
150 ml (5 fl oz) pure (pouring) cream (35% fat), whipped

GARNISH
1 pineapple, cut into 1 cm (⅜ inch) cubes
1 mango, peeled, deseeded and thinly sliced
4 passionfruit
1 handful of baby coriander (cilantro)
100 g (3½ oz) mango pearls (see glossary)

Preheat the oven to 160°C (315°F). Line a 30 cm (12 inch) square baking tray with baking paper and spray with cooking spray or oil.

In the clean bowl of an electric mixer fitted with the whisk attachment, whisk the egg whites for 2–3 minutes to soft peaks. Reduce speed to low, then gradually add the caster sugar and cornflour together until combined, then gradually add the vanilla paste. The meringue should be thick and glossy.

Spread the meringue evenly over the baking paper, taking it right to the edges. Bake for 15 minutes or until a light golden colour. Don't open the door while cooking.

Sprinkle the extra caster sugar over a fresh sheet of baking paper on a flat surface. Turn the cooked meringue onto the sugar-dusted paper. Flip the paper over onto a clean tray and gently peel the baking paper away. Cool at room temperature.

To make the mango crème pâtissiere, put the mango purée, milk and vanilla seeds into a medium saucepan over medium–low heat and bring just to the boil. Remove from the heat.

Meanwhile, whisk the egg yolks, custard powder and sugar in a medium bowl until thick and pale.

Gradually whisk a little of the hot liquid into the egg mixture. Return the saucepan to the heat and bring to the boil. Add the egg mixture to the remaining hot milk mixture, whisking constantly over medium heat until the custard comes to the boil.

Remove from the heat and transfer to a bowl, lay plastic wrap on the surface of the crème pâtissiere to prevent a skin forming. When the crème has cooled to 28°C (82°F) or just above room temperature before using.

When ready to assemble, whisk the crème pâtissiere and gently add in the whipped cream to lighten. Use a spatula to spread the custard evenly over the meringue.

Gently roll the meringue, starting from one edge, to form a tight roll. Transfer to a platter and chill until ready to serve.

Just before serving, garnish the roulade with the tropical fruit and the mango pearls for that extra pop in the mouth. Scatter with baby coriander.

3SOME TWIST
Make the meringue sheet in advance and store in a dry, cool area, wrapped in plastic wrap, for up to 24 hours. Make sure you remove the meringue from the baking paper as soon as you've sugared it, otherwise it will stick.

A fun creation: instead of a traditional pavlova, I've gone ahead and built it in sections. Build it three blocks tall and you can take them down and share with friends at the table.

Note: You'll need clear stackable containers to serve this dish, but if you can't find them you could simply layer the elements in a tall glass jar or vase like a regular trifle.

———

MAKES 1 STACK

———

PAVLOVA

2 egg whites from 60 g (large) eggs, at room temperature

60 g (2¼ oz) caster (superfine) sugar

1 pinch of cream of tartar

30 g (1 oz/¼ cup) pure icing (confectioners') sugar, sifted

1 handful of baby coriander (cilantro) leaves, to serve

MANGO AND PASSIONFRUIT JELLY

100 ml (3½ fl oz) passionfruit purée (see glossary)

275 ml (9½ fl oz) mango purée (see glossary)

40 g (1½ oz) caster (superfine) sugar

2 sheets titanium-strength gelatine, softened in cold water

DIPLOMAT CREAM

250 ml (9 fl oz/1 cup) milk

1 vanilla bean, split and seeds scraped

4 egg yolks

60 g (¼ cup) caster (superfine) sugar

30 g (1 oz) custard powder

25 g (1 oz) unsalted butter, softened

125 ml (4½ fl oz/½ cup) pure (pouring) cream (35% fat)

TROPICAL COMPOTE

½ pineapple

2 mangoes

100 g (3½ oz) mango pearls (see glossary)

3 passionfruit

———

Preheat the oven to 60°C (140°F) and line a baking tray with baking paper.

Put the egg whites in a clean dry bowl. In an electric mixer fitted with the whisk attachment, whisk on high speed until soft peaks form. Reduce the speed and gradually add the caster sugar and cream of tartar, whisking well after each addition.

Return to high speed and whisk until the meringue is thick and glossy and the sugar has dissolved. To test, rub a little meringue between your fingers. If it is still gritty, continue to whisk. Firm peaks need to be achieved.

Remove the bowl from the mixer and fold in the icing sugar until completely combined. Be quick or the meringue will become runny.

Using 2 large spoons, form quenelles of meringue and place them on the prepared tray. They do not have to be perfect; spike it up. Transfer to the oven and bake for 2 hours.

Turn off the heat and allow the pavlovas to cool in the oven for 1–2 hours. Do not open the door until the oven has completely cooled. Keep checking to make sure the temperature isn't too high: you do not want the meringues to gain any colour.

When completely cooled, store meringues in an airtight container until required.

To make the mango and passionfruit jelly, combine the fruit purées and sugar in a small saucepan over medium heat and bring just to the boil. Remove from the heat.

Squeeze gelatine gently to remove excess liquid and stir into the hot mixture. Strain through a fine sieve into a plastic container. Lay a piece of plastic wrap on the surface of the jelly and allow to cool.

When the jelly has cooled down, place the first glass for the stack on a tray lined with plastic wrap and pour the jelly into the glass. Carefully transfer to the refrigerator for about 2 hours to set. Reserve until required for assembly.

To make the diplomat cream, put the milk in a medium saucepan. Scrape the seeds from the vanilla bean directly into the milk. Bring to the boil then remove from the heat.

Whisk the egg yolks and sugar together until well combined, then stir through the custard powder.

Pour a little of the hot milk mixture over the egg mixture. Whisk to combine, then pour the egg mixture into the saucepan with the remaining hot milk mixture. Cook over medium heat for 5–8 minutes, whisking until thickened.

Remove from the heat and transfer to an electric mixer fitted with the paddle attachment. Beat until cool. When cooled to about 40°C (104°F) or just above body temperature, gradually add the butter.

Transfer 250 g (9 oz) of the diplomat cream to a clean bowl and use an electric mixer fitted with the whisk attachment to whisk it until it is smooth and lump-free. Reduce the speed and add the cream, continuing to whisk until the mixture is soft.

To prepare the tropical compote, peel and core the pineapple, making sure not to take too much of the flesh off with the skin. Cut the flesh into 1 cm (⅜ inch) cubes and put them into a small bowl.

Drain excess syrup from the mango pearls and add the pearls to the pineapple mixture.

Cut the passionfruit in half and scrape the pulp and the seeds into a separate small bowl. Stir the passionfruit pulp to help break it down, make sure there are no white bits. Add the pulp to the pineapple mixture. Peel and deseed the mango, chop into small cubes and add it to the pineapple mixture. Set aside in the refrigerator until needed for assembly.

To assemble, stack the second glass on top of the glass with the jelly. Break up the meringue and fill the second glass with meringue pieces, then spoon the diplomat cream on top, filling to 1 cm (⅜ inch) from the top of the glass.

Stack the final glass on top and fill with the tropical compote. Garnish with baby coriander.

Sharing is caring. **Deconstruct** a pavlova, pile it in **the centre of the table** and share it **with your loved ones.**

_____

3SOME TWIST
This dessert is something you can prepare ahead and put it together at the last minute.

FROZEN PAV SANDWICH

Eton Mess can't get any better than when it's transformed into an ice-cream sandwich. Most ice-cream sandwiches have a biscuit base, but I made this with meringue for a lighter texture. Make these in advance, ready for unexpected visitors on summer days. I've used ready-made ice cream for this recipe to make it simple.

SERVES 6

PAVLOVA MERINGUE
4 egg whites
1 teaspoon cream of tartar
100 g (3½ oz) caster (superfine) sugar
50 g (1¾ oz) icing (confectioners') sugar, sifted

ICE-CREAM RIPPLE
500 g (1 lb 2 oz) vanilla ice cream
250 g (9 oz) raspberry sorbet

Preheat the oven to 80°C (175°F). Line 2 baking trays with baking paper. On each sheet of baking paper, use a 7 cm (2¾ inch) circle cutter and a black marker pen to draw 6 evenly-spaced circles. Turn the paper over so you can see the circles but the ink is underneath. This is to help shape the meringues.

Using an electric mixer fitted with the whisk attachment, whisk the egg whites and cream of tartar to medium peaks. Reduce the speed and gradually add the caster sugar, whisking to firm peak stage. Remove from the mixer and gradually fold in the icing sugar.

Divide the meringue into 2 equal portions. Using a plain 12 mm piping (icing) nozzle, pipe the meringue into the marked circles, using a circular motion and working outwards from the centre.

Bake for 2–3 hours until dry and crunchy, but don't allow the meringue to colour. Set aside to cool completely, then store in an airtight container until needed.

To make the ice-cream ripple, put the ice cream in a bowl and set aside to soften. Gently fold the raspberry sorbet through to create a ripple effect. Return it to the freezer for about 5 minutes.

Cut out a 10 cm square of plastic wrap for each of six 7 cm (2¾ inch) egg rings and lay them on a tray, then fold the edges of the plastic wrap over into the middle of the ring. Cut a strip of baking paper and line the inside of each ring.

Spoon in the ice-cream ripple, making sure it's level. Return to the freezer for at least 30 minutes until solid.

To assemble just before serving, remove the ice cream from the egg ring and sandwich between two meringues.

3SOME TWIST
Change the flavours up, or use a jam as a substitute for the raspberry sorbet. The meringue discs can be made in advance and stored in an airtight container for 1–2 weeks.

It's all about elegance: pretty little cakes that are small enough — just a couple of bites — so you don't feel guilty having more than one of them, plus the best scones you'll ever have in your life!

A gluten-free afternoon tea item that's light, good-looking and refreshing.

SERVES 20

COCONUT DACQUOISE
75 g (2¾ oz) almond meal, sifted
135 g (4¾ oz) icing (confectioners') sugar, sifted
40 g (1½ oz) desiccated (finely shredded) coconut
5 egg whites
50g (1¾ oz) caster (superfine) sugar

Preheat the oven to 140°C (275°F). Spray twenty small 6 cm (2¼ inch) round tart rings with baking spray and set them out on a baking tray lined with baking paper.

In a small bowl, mix together the sifted almond meal, icing sugar and coconut. Set aside.

In an electric mixer fitted with the whisk attachment, whisk the egg whites on medium to high speed until they start to form soft peaks. Gradually add the caster sugar. Increase the speed to high for about 3–5 minutes until firm peaks form, the meringue is glossy, and the sugar has all dissolved.

Remove from the machine and use a spatula to fold in the sifted dry ingredients.

Put the dacquoise mixture into a piping (icing) bag fitted with a size 9 plain nozzle. Pipe the mixture into the rings, starting from the middle and working in a swirling motion out to the edge of the ring.

Bake for 20–25 minutes until the dacquoise has a light golden colour and feels firm to touch. Cool in the tin and set aside until ready to assemble.

CALAMANSI LIME CREMEUX
70 ml (2¼ fl oz) calamansi (Chinese orange) purée (see glossary)
2 eggs
100 (3½ oz) caster (superfine) sugar
1 sheet titanium-strength gelatine, softened in cold water
145 g (5¼ oz) unsalted butter, at room temperature
1 teaspoon lime zest

Put the calamansi purée in a small saucepan and bring to the boil over medium heat.

Meanwhile, whisk together the eggs and caster sugar in a medium bowl.

Pour the boiling purée into the egg mixture and whisk until combined. Return to the saucepan over medium heat, whisking constantly until the mixture reaches 86°C (187°F) – use a sugar thermometer to measure. Remove the saucepan from the heat.

Squeeze the gelatine to remove excess water and stir into the hot mixture until completely dissolved. Strain the curd through a fine sieve.

Cool the curd to 34°C (93°F) or just below body temperature. Use a hand blender to beat the butter into the curd for 2–3 minutes, until it is smooth and silky. Stir in the lime zest.

Transfer the curd to a container and cover the surface with plastic wrap. Refrigerate until needed for assembly.

COMPRESSED PINEAPPLE

50 g (1¾ oz) caster (superfine) sugar

155 g (5½ oz) fresh pineapple

5 cm (2 inch) piece of fresh ginger

1 teaspoon finely chopped fresh coriander
    (cilantro) leaves

In a small saucepan, bring the sugar and 50 ml
(1¾ fl oz) of water to the boil over high heat. Remove
from the heat and allow to cool.

Remove the skin from the pineapple and cut into
1 x 3 cm (⅜ x 1¼ inch) batons.

Grate the fresh ginger, wrap in muslin
(cheesecloth) and squeeze out the juice.

In a medium bowl, combine all of the ingredients
and carefully mix together. Transfer to a vacuum
pack bag and remove the air using a vacuum pack
machine. If you don't have vacuum equipment, just
use an airtight container.

Lay the pineapple flat in the refrigerator
until needed.

———————

TO ASSEMBLE

100 g (3½ oz) non-melting icing (confectioners')
    sugar (see glossary)

1 small handful of baby coriander (cilantro) sprigs

50 ml (1¾ fl oz) BRUSH ME PRETTY nappage
    (see page 232)

Strain the pineapple mixture and discard the syrup.

Lay out the dacquoise discs on a tray and dust
with the icing sugar.

Put the calamansi cremeux in a piping (icing) bag
fitted with a small plain nozzle. Pipe approximately
2 teaspoons of cremeux in the centre of each
dacquoise disc.

Heat the nappage until very hot and runny. Add it
to the drained pineapple in a bowl and mix until the
pineapple is well coated.

Place 4–5 pineapple batons on top of the cremeux
in a loose pile. Garnish with the baby coriander.

———————

HIGH LIFE TWIST

Try not to overcook the dacquoise; it should be
light and fluffy.

I was inspired to create
this by Pierre Hermé
and have put it on my
afternoon tea menu.
It works well with many
different types of tea.

SPIKE PAGE 206

When Spike featured on Instagram my fans said that it looked like my hair! I just thought it looked sexy. A yoghurt lime cremeux is inserted in a ball of glazed mousse and decorated with crunchy meringue kisses.

MAKES 20

MERINGUE KISSES

60 g (2¼ oz) egg whites, at room temperature
60 g (2¼ oz) caster (superfine) sugar
30 g (1 oz/¼ cup) pure icing (confectioners') sugar, sifted

Preheat a dehydrator to 60°C (140°F) or an oven to 40°C (104°F). Line two dehydrator trays or baking trays with baking paper.

Put the egg whites in the clean dry bowl of an electric mixer fitted with the whisk attachment. Beat on a high speed for 3–5 minutes, until soft peaks form. Reduce the speed to medium and gradually add the caster sugar, until all the sugar is combined.

Return to high speed and whisk until the meringue is thick and glossy and the sugar has dissolved. Rub a little meringue between your fingers. If it is still gritty with sugar, continue to whisk until the mixture no longer feels gritty.

Use a large metal spoon to fold in the sifted icing sugar.

Put the meringue in a piping (icing) bag fitted with a plain size 9 or 10 nozzle. Pipe 2.5 cm (1 inch) wide meringue kisses onto the prepared trays. You'll need about 150 tiny kisses.

Put in the dehydrator for 3 hours or in the oven overnight or until the kisses are completely dry. Cool on the tray, then store in an airtight container until required.

SABLE BISCUIT

50 g (1¾ oz) icing (confectioners') sugar
75 g (2¾ oz) unsalted butter, at room temperature
1 egg
½ vanilla bean, seeds scraped
150 g (5½ oz/1 cup) plain (all-purpose) flour, sifted

Put the icing sugar and butter in the bowl of an electric mixer fitted with the paddle attachment and start beating on low speed. Increase to medium speed and beat until pale and creamy.

While still beating, add the egg, then the vanilla seeds and the sifted flour until a smooth dough forms.

Gather the dough into a ball. Shape into a flat rectangle, wrap in plastic wrap and refrigerate for at least 4 hours.

Preheat the oven to 160°C (315°F). Line a baking tray with baking paper.

On a lightly floured work surface, roll the chilled dough out to 5 mm (¼ inch) thickness. Use a 3 cm (1¼ inch) round cutter to cut 20 small discs.

Transfer the discs to the prepared tray and bake for 15–20 minutes until golden. Cool on the tray and reserve in an airtight container until needed.

BLUEBERRY GLAZE

260 ml (9¼ fl oz) blueberry purée
250 g (9 oz) caster (superfine) sugar
100 g (3½ oz) trimoline (see glossary)
100 ml (3½ fl oz) glucose syrup
8 sheets titanium-strength gelatine, softened in cold water
100 g (3½ oz) cocoa butter

Combine the blueberry purée, caster sugar, trimoline and glucose syrup in a medium saucepan over medium heat. Use a thermometer to measure when the mixture reaches 70°C (158°F).

Remove from the heat. Squeeze excess water out of the gelatine and whisk in the gelatine and cocoa butter.

Pass through a fine sieve into a container, laying plastic wrap on the surface to prevent a skin forming. Chill in the refrigerator for at least 24 hours.

YOGHURT MOUSSE

2 teaspoons caster (superfine) sugar

2 teaspoons lime juice

1 sheet titanium-strength gelatine, softened in cold water

60 g (2¼ oz) plain yoghurt

60 ml (2 fl oz/¼ cup) pure (pouring) cream (35% fat), lightly whisked

Combine the sugar and lime juice in a small saucepan and bring to the boil over medium heat. Remove from the heat.

Squeeze excess water out of the gelatine and stir through the hot syrup. Cool.

Whisk the lime jelly mixture into the yoghurt, then gently fold the cream through.

Transfer the mousse mixture to a piping (icing) bag. Set two sheets of 20 silicone sphere moulds measuring 3.5 cm (1½ inch) in diameter on trays and pipe the mousse into the moulds.

Freeze until needed.

––––––––––

BLUEBERRY MOUSSE

160 ml (5¼ fl oz) blueberry purée (see glossary)

1 sheet titanium-strength gelatine, softened in cold water

80 g (2¾ oz) white chocolate (28%), chopped or buttons

170 ml (5½ fl oz/⅔ cup) pure (pouring) cream (35%), lightly whisked

In a small saucepan, bring the blueberry purée just to the boil. Remove from the heat.

Squeeze excess water from the gelatine and stir it into the boiling purée until completely combined.

Put the white chocolate into a medium heatproof bowl and use a fine sieve to strain the purée over the chocolate. Stir to combine, making sure all the chocolate is melted. Cover the surface with plastic wrap and cool to 40°C (104°F) or just above body temperature.

Meanwhile, lay two sheets of twenty 4.5 cm (1¾ inch) diameter sphere moulds on trays and set aside.

When the berry mixture has cooled, fold in the lightly whisked cream.

Put the blueberry mousse in a piping (icing) bag. Remove the 3.5 cm yoghurt mousse moulds from the freezer and release the domes from the moulds.

Pipe the blueberry mousse halfway up the side of each 4.5 cm mould and place a yoghurt mousse dome in the centre, pushing it down gently so that the mousse comes up the sides and is level at the top but not overflowing.

Freeze, making sure the tray is completely level, for 2–3 hours or until firm.

––––––––––

TO ASSEMBLE

When ready to glaze, heat the glaze to 45°C (113°F) in the microwave. Slowly stir the mixture until it cools down to 40°C (104°F) and is smooth. Set aside.

Remove the frozen mousse domes from the moulds. Use your hands to slightly soften the flat surfaces of two of the domes and then stick them together to assemble a sphere. Place the sphere on a wire rack set over a tray. Work quickly so the mousse doesn't start to melt. Repeat with the remaining domes.

Pour the warm glaze over the domes to completely cover. Allow the excess glaze to drip off the dome and then carefully transfer each dome onto a vanilla sable biscuit.

Use a skewer and palette knife to transfer the domes to a serving plate. Apply the meringue kisses around the ball, making sure the spikes are facing out.

––––––––––

HIGH LIFE TWIST

Make sure the mousse is frozen solid so that the glaze sticks to it. Assemble the spheres, glaze them and store them in the freezer for up to 1 week, then add the meringue kisses to serve.

These scones are a winner, people come to the hotel before 11am waiting for them, or double their order to take them away. I bake them twice for 11am and then again at 2pm, as we have afternoon tea until 5pm. Soak the sultanas up to a week ahead, ready to make the scones.

———————

SERVES 15–20

———————

400 g (14 oz/2⅔ cups) plain (all-purpose) flour, plus extra for dusting
50 g (1¾ oz) caster (superfine) sugar
1 tablespoon baking powder
120 g (4¼ oz) unsalted butter, at room temperature
2 eggs
160 ml (5¼ fl oz) buttermilk
1 teaspoon vanilla bean paste
1 egg yolk, whisked

EARL GREY TEA SULTANAS
3 teaspoons loose leaf Earl Grey tea
100 g (3½ oz) sultanas (golden raisins)

———————

In a small saucepan, bring 250ml (9 fl oz/1 cup) of water to the boil over high heat. Remove the saucepan from the heat and add the tea leaves. Stir while infusing for 3 minutes. Strain the tea through a fine sieve, reserving the liquid and discarding the tea leaves.

Put the sultanas in a heatproof bowl. Pour the tea over the sultanas, cool and store in the refrigerator covered with plastic wrap until needed. You can keep the sultanas soaking in the tea for up to 1 week.

To make the scones, put the dry ingredients in the bowl of an electric mixer fitted with the paddle attachment. Add a pinch of salt and the butter, then beat on low speed for 5 minutes until the mixture is crumbly.

Whisk together the eggs, buttermilk and vanilla bean paste. Gradually add this mixture to the flour mixture. Mix on high speed for 2–3 minutes, until the

dough comes together and there are no crumbs in the bottom of the bowl.

Turn the dough out onto a lightly floured work surface and divide it into two halves. Gently knead one portion of dough into a rectangle shape and cover with plastic wrap. Set aside to rest for 10 minutes.

Lightly knead the sultanas into the remaining dough portion, form into a rectangle shape and cover with plastic wrap. Set aside to rest for 10 minutes.

Preheat the oven to 190°C (375°F). Lightly spray two baking trays with baking spray.

Roll out each dough portion to a thickness of 2 cm (¾ inch). Use a 5.5 cm (2¼ inch) circle cutter to cut out discs. Try not to touch the dough, as this makes it shrink: just hold the side of the cutter ring and push down.

Arrange the scones, flat-side up, on the prepared baking trays. Brush the tops of the sultana scones with the egg yolk and lightly dust the tops of the plain scones with the extra plain flour. Set aside for 1 hour to allow the gluten to relax.

Bake the scones for 15 minutes, until just golden. Wait a couple of minutes, then eat them straight away, served with clotted cream and your favourite jam.

———————

HIGH LIFE TWIST
I always give each scone a pat as I place it on the tray: I believe the extra TLC helps them rise better. High heat is a must, as you want them to cook quickly; slightly undercook them, as they continue cooking once out of the oven.

A different way to present a tart for afternoon tea.

SERVES 8

---

450 g (1 lb) fresh raspberries

SABLE BASQUE
3 egg yolks
100 g (3½ oz) caster (superfine) sugar
100 g (3½ oz) unsalted butter, at room temperature
145 g (5¼ oz) strong flour, sifted
2 teaspoons baking powder, sifted

LEMON AND PASSIONFRUIT CURD
50 ml (1¾ fl oz) lemon juice
50 ml (1¾ fl oz) passionfruit purée (see glossary)
3 eggs, plus 1 egg yolk extra
130 g (4½ oz) caster (superfine) sugar
45 g (1½ oz) unsalted butter, at room temperature
finely grated zest of 1 lemon

ITALIAN MERINGUE
220 g (7¾ oz/1 cup) caster (superfine) sugar
4 egg whites

In a small bowl, whisk together the egg yolks and caster sugar.

Using an electric mixer fitted with the paddle attachment, beat the butter on low speed, for 3–4 minutes until light and fluffy. Do not overbeat.

Add half the egg mixture and beat until combined. Stop the machine and scrape down the side of the bowl.

Return to low speed and add half the flour and baking powder. Add the rest of the egg mixture and then the remaining flour. Add a generous pinch of salt. Stop the machine and scrape down the side of the bowl, then mix until combined.

Turn the dough out onto a piece of plastic wrap and form into a rectangle. Wrap in the plastic and refrigerate overnight.

Preheat the oven to 160°C (315°F). Line a baking tray with baking paper. Remove the dough from the refrigerator. On a lightly floured surface, roll to a thickness of 1 cm (⅜ inch) and use a 5 cm (2 inch) round cutter to cut out 8 discs.

Place the discs on the prepared tray and bake for 8–10 minutes until light golden brown. Cool on the tray and reserve until needed.

To make the lemon and passionfruit curd, bring the lemon juice and passionfruit purée to the boil in a medium saucepan over medium heat.

Meanwhile, whisk together the eggs, egg yolk and caster sugar in a heatproof bowl. Pour the boiling fruit mixture into the egg mixture and whisk until combined. Pour the mixture back into the saucepan and return to medium heat, whisking constantly until a thermometer reads 86°C (187°F).

Remove from the heat and strain the curd through a fine sieve. Cool the curd to 34°C (93°F).

Use a handheld blender to blend the butter into the curd for 2–3 minutes, until smooth and silky. Add the lemon zest and stir to combine.

Transfer the curd into a container and cover the surface with plastic wrap. Reserve in the refrigerator.

To make the meringue, put the sugar in a small saucepan with enough water to make a slurry. Cook over high heat, until a thermometer reads 121°C (250°F).

Meanwhile, put the egg whites in the bowl of an electric mixer fitted with the whisk attachment. When the syrup reaches 118°C (244°F), turn on to high speed.

Reduce the speed to low as you gradually pour in the hot syrup. Return to high speed and whisk until cold and the meringue is thick and glossy.

Put the lemon curd in a piping (icing) bag fitted with a large plain nozzle. Pipe a bulb of lemon curd on to each sable basque, arrange raspberries around the outer edge of the tart, then fill the centre space with more lemon curd.

Transfer the meringue to a piping (icing) bag fitted with a St Honore nozzle (see glossary). Pipe an S-shaped swirl of Italian meringue on top. Use a blowtorch to lightly caramelise the meringue.

HIGH LIFE TWIST
The sable basque mixture will be sticky (you'll need to flour the bench) and must rest overnight before baking; however, it can only rest for one night in the refrigerator or it will not react as it should.

I wanted to add a little green tea into my afternoon tea in honour of my many Asian fans around the world. This cake is playing on a club sandwich.

MAKES 40

WHITE CHOCOLATE CHANTILLY CREAM

600 ml (21 fl oz) pure (pouring) cream (35% fat)
1 vanilla bean, split and seeds scraped
300 g (10½ oz) white chocolate (28%), chopped or buttons
4 sheets titanium-strength gelatine, softened in cold water

Combine the cream with the vanilla bean and seeds in a small saucepan and bring just to the boil over medium heat.

Meanwhile, put the chocolate in a heatproof bowl. Squeeze excess liquid out of the gelatine.

Remove the boiling cream from the heat and stir in the gelatine, then pour the hot mixture over the chocolate. Stir until all the chocolate has melted.

Transfer to a container and cover the surface with plastic wrap or freezer film. Refrigerate overnight.

STRAWBERRY JELLY (gelatine)

350 ml (12 fl oz) strawberry purée (see glossary)
55 g (2 oz/¼ cup) caster (superfine) sugar
4 sheets titanium-strength gelatine, softened in cold water

Line a 30 x 40 cm (12 x 16 inch) baking tin with plastic wrap and set aside.

Combine the strawberry purée and sugar in a small saucepan with 300 ml (10½ fl oz) of water and bring just to the boil over medium heat.

Squeeze the gelatine to remove excess water and stir into the boiling purée mixture. Strain into a container and lay plastic wrap on the surface of the liquid. Allow to cool to 30°C (86°F).

Pour the jelly into the prepared tray. Carefully transfer to the freezer for at least 1 hour to set.

MATCHA SPONGE

7 eggs
220 g (7¾ oz/1 cup) caster (superfine) sugar
220 g (7¾ oz) plain (all-purpose) flour, sifted
3 teaspoons matcha (powdered green tea), sifted

Preheat the oven to 160°C (315°F). Lightly spray a 30 x 60 cm (12 x 24 inch) baking tray with baking spray and line with baking paper.

In an electric mixer fitted with the whisk attachment, whisk together the eggs and sugar on high speed until light and fluffy and doubled in volume.

Use a spatula to fold in the sifted flour, until just combined.

Fold in the matcha powder, making sure not to overmix or the sponge will break down.

Pour the mixture onto the prepared tray and use a palette knife to spread it evenly.

Bake for 15 minutes, or until a skewer inserted into the centre of the cake comes out clean.

When you remove it from the oven, immediately use the baking paper to slide it off the baking tray to prevent it cooking any further. Transfer to a wire rack to cool and reserve until needed.

300 g (10½ oz) strawberries, hulled and thinly sliced

Lay a piece of baking paper on top of the matcha sponge and flip it over. Remove the baking paper that the sponge was baked on. Cut the sponge into thirds and place one of the pieces on a cutting board.

Lightly whip the White Chocolate Chantilly Cream. Use a palette knife to evenly spread 100 g (3½ oz) onto the sponge.

Remove the jelly from the freezer and take it out of the tray. Trim the jelly into a 20 x 30 cm (8 x 12 inch) rectangle and lay the jelly on top of the chantilly cream.

Spread another 100 g (3½ oz) of Chantilly cream on top of the jelly and then place a second matcha sponge rectangle on top.

Lay the thinly sliced strawberries onto the sponge and spread the rest of the Chantilly cream evenly over the strawberries.

Finish off the sandwich with the last matcha sponge rectangle. Make sure all the layers line up and transfer to the refrigerator to set for at least 30 minutes.

When ready to serve, cut the sandwich into 6 cm (2½ inch) wide strips. Then cut each strip into four 5 cm (2 inch) long rectangles. Carefully cut diagonally through the middle of each rectangle to form triangles.

———————

HIGH LIFE TWIST
Make sure the strawberries are perfectly ripe, the layers are all level and don't overcook the sponge.

Who needs a club sandwich when you can have a **matcha club cake?** Turning savoury to sweet; **traditional to modern.**

Pierre Hermé is one of the great pâtissiers, and after I won best dessert in the UK I was lucky enough to work a stint with him in Paris, where I learned about the beauty of patisserie. This recipe is one that uses what I learned. I leave out the nuts to satisfy guests with allergies.

SERVES 75–80

BROWNIE BASE

240 g (8¾ oz) dark chocolate (55%), chopped or buttons
180 g (6¼ oz) unsalted butter, at room temperature
300 g (10½ oz) caster (superfine) sugar
4 eggs
180 g (6¼ oz) plain (all-purpose) flour, sifted
½ teaspoon baking powder

Preheat the oven to 180°C (350°F). Line a 30 cm (12 inch) square cake tin with baking paper,

In a medium microwave-proof bowl melt the chocolate and butter in 30-second bursts, stirring between each burst, until smooth. Set aside.

In an electric mixer fitted with the whisk attachment, whisk the caster sugar and eggs on high speed for 3–4 minutes until fluffy, glossy and doubled in volume.

Reduce the speed to low and add the sifted flour and baking powder. Once incorporated, add the chocolate mixture. Continue whisking until well combined.

Use a palette knife to spread the mixture evenly onto the prepared tray.

Bake for 20–30 minutes until set. A skewer inserted in the centre should come out a little gooey.

Lay baking paper on top and use a palette knife to push the mixture up to the edges so that the surface is completely flat.

CHOCOLATE ANGLAISE

125 ml (4½ fl oz/½ cup) milk
125 ml (4½ fl oz/½ cup) cream
1 vanilla bean, split and seeds scraped
60 g (2¼ oz) caster (superfine) sugar
3 egg yolks
2½ sheets titanium-strength gelatine, softened in cold water
90 g (3¼ oz) dark chocolate, chopped or buttons

Combine the milk, cream, vanilla bean and seeds in a medium saucepan over medium heat and bring to the boil.

Meanwhile, whisk together the caster (superfine) sugar and the egg yolks in a small heatproof bowl until completely combined.

Discard the vanilla bean and pour half of the hot milk mixture into the egg mixture. Whisk to combine. Transfer the egg mixture back to the saucepan with the remaining milk mixture over medium heat. Stir the anglaise constantly and use a thermometer to measure when it reaches 84°C (183°F), or is thick and coats the back of a spoon.

Remove the anglaise from the heat. Squeeze out excess water from the gelatine and stir it into the anglaise.

Put the chocolate in a bowl. Strain the custard mixture through a fine sieve over the chocolate. Whisk until completely combined. Lay plastic wrap on the surface of the anglaise and allow to cool to 40°C (104°F) or just above body temperature.

Pour the cooled anglaise on top of the chocolate brownie base. Lay flat in the freezer overnight so that the anglaise sets.

CHOCOLATE GANACHE

220 ml (7½ fl oz) pure (pouring) cream (35% fat)
1 tablespoon trimoline (see glossary), optional
180 g (6¼ oz) dark chocolate, chopped or buttons
70 g (2½ oz) unsalted butter, at room temperature

Combine the cream and the trimoline, if using, in a small saucepan over medium heat and bring to the boil. Remove from the heat.

Put the chocolate in a heatproof bowl. Pour the hot cream over the chocolate and use a handheld blender to blend the ganache until smooth.

Lay plastic wrap on the surface of the ganache and allow to cool to 40°C (104°F) or just above body temperature. Remove the plastic wrap from the surface and use a handheld blender to blend in the butter.

Transfer to a clean dry container and cover with plastic wrap to prevent a skin forming. Keep the ganache at room temperature to set overnight.

_____

DARK CHOCOLATE RECTANGLES

300 g (10½ oz) dark chocolate (55%), tempered
    (see page 232)

Line a flat tray with an acetate sheet. Use a palette knife to spread a thin layer of the tempered chocolate on the acetate.

Allow the chocolate to just set, and then cut 1.5 x 7 cm (⅝ x 2¾ inch) strips.

When the chocolate has completely set, lay a piece of baking paper on top and then place a dry flat tray on top. Refrigerate for 10 minutes.

Remove from the refrigerator and turn the trays over, so that the shiny side of the chocolate is on top. Remove the tray and also the acetate sheet. Reserve at room temperature until needed.

_____

TO ASSEMBLE

Transfer the frozen brownie to a cutting board. Cut the brownie into 1.5 x 7 cm (⅝ x 2¾ inch) strips.

Put the chocolate ganache in a piping (icing) bag fitted with a size 4 plain nozzle, pipe balls of chocolate ganache on top starting from one end and working to the other.

Carefully lay a chocolate rectangle on top of each brownie.

_____

HIGH LIFE TWIST

One key thing is to be sure to cook out the anglaise, don't just rely on the gelatine for the stability. Make sure to keep everything level. The brownie and anglaise base can be stored in the freezer for 2 weeks. You can add nuts to the brownie mixture if you like.

I've kept this **chocoholic's delight** on the **afternoon tea menu** from day one and even **changed it up for functions** as a plated dessert and **a whole cake too.**

BROWNIES PAGE 216

Try this flourless chocolate sponge roll with chocolate mousse and chocolate glaze, finished with chocolate sheets. It's always on the afternoon tea menu because it's gluten free and perfect for chocolate lovers.

MAKES 14

CHOCOLATE GLAZE

125 ml (4½ fl oz/½ cup) pure (pouring) cream (35% fat)
150 ml (5 fl oz) glucose syrup (see glossary)
180 g (6¼ oz) caster (superfine) sugar
55 g (2 oz/½ cup) cocoa powder (unsweetened), sifted
4 sheets titanium-strength gelatine, softened in cold water

Put the cream, glucose, sugar and 50 ml (1¾ fl oz) of water into a small saucepan over medium heat and bring to the boil.

Remove from the heat and stir in the cocoa. Return to the heat and boil, whisking until smooth.

Pour the glaze into a stainless steel bowl. Using a handheld blender, blend until completely combined and smooth.

Squeeze excess water from the gelatine and add it to the glaze. Continue to blend, until well combined and smooth.

Strain the mixture through a fine sieve into a container. Lay plastic wrap on the surface and refrigerate overnight.

CHOCOLATE MOUSSE

75 g (2¾ oz) dark chocolate (63%), chopped or buttons
55 g (2 oz/¼ cup) caster (superfine) sugar
1 egg, plus 1 yolk extra
90 ml (3 fl oz) pure (pouring) cream (35% fat), lightly whisked

Put the chocolate in a microwave-proof bowl and melt in 30-second bursts, stirring between each burst, until completely melted. Cool to 40°C (104°F).

Combine the sugar and 25 ml (1 fl oz) of water in a small saucepan over high heat, brushing the side of the saucepan with a wet pastry brush to prevent burning. Use a thermometer to measure when the syrup reaches 121°C (250°F).

Meanwhile, whisk the egg and egg yolk using an electric mixer fitted with the whisk attachment. Whisk on high speed until light and pale.

When the sugar syrup is the correct temperature, reduce the mixer to medium speed. Gradually pour in the hot sugar syrup, avoiding the whisk and side of the bowl.

Increase to high speed and whisk until the egg mixture (pâte de bombe) has cooled down. Take the bowl off the mixer and fold in the melted chocolate by hand. Be quick or the chocolate will set and lumps will form.

Once all the chocolate has been combined, fold through the lightly whisked cream until completely combined. Cover with plastic wrap and refrigerate for at least 1 hour to firm up.

CHOCOLATE FLOURLESS SPONGE

5 eggs, separated, yolks lightly beaten
110 g (3¾ oz/½ cup) caster (superfine) sugar
40 g (1½ oz/⅓ cup) cocoa powder
(unsweetened), sifted

Preheat the oven to 190°C (375°F). Line a 40 cm (16 inch) square baking tray with baking paper. Spray with canola oil.

Whisk the egg whites in the clean bowl of an electric mixer fitted with the whisk attachment, on high speed for 3–5 minutes until soft peaks form. Reduce to low speed and gradually add the caster sugar. Increase to high speed for 3–5 minutes, whisking until the meringue is thick and glossy.

Remove from the mixer and fold through the sifted cocoa and then the egg yolks. Use a spatula, making sure to fold all ingredients through gently to stop the meringue from collapsing.

Spread the chocolate sponge mixture evenly over the prepared tray, taking it right to the edge. Bake for 6–8 minutes, until it springs back when you touch it.

Slide the sponge on the baking paper onto a wire rack to cool.

――――――

DARK CHOCOLATE SHARDS

300 g (10½ oz) dark chocolate (55%), tempered
(see page 232)

Line a flat tray with an acetate sheet or cellophane. Use a palette knife to spread a thin layer of the tempered chocolate onto the acetate.

When the chocolate has completely set, lay baking paper and then a dry flat tray on top.

Refrigerate for 10 minutes. Remove the trays from the refrigerator and turn them over, so that the shiny side of the chocolate is on top. Remove the tray and the acetate sheet. Break the chocolate into pieces approximately 4 cm (1½ inches) across.

――――――

TO ASSEMBLE

Lay another piece of paper on top of the sponge. Carefully flip the sponge over and remove the baking paper that the sponge was baked on.

Use a spatula to spread chocolate mousse evenly over the sponge. Use the baking paper to help you roll the sponge with the mousse, making it as tight as possible.

Transfer the roulade to the freezer to firm for a couple of hours.

Heat the chocolate glaze to 33°C (91°F) or just below body temperature and place the roulade, seam side down, on a wire rack over a tray. Pour the glaze on top of the roulade, making sure there are no areas of sponge left exposed.

Line a tray with baking paper and spray the paper with baking spray. Carefully place the roulade onto the tray and freeze just until the glaze has set.

Transfer the glazed roulade to a cutting board and cut 2.5 cm (1 inch) thick slices. Apply shards of broken chocolate around the top of each slice.

――――――

HIGH LIFE TWIST

The sponge can be stored in the freezer for up to 2 weeks; when you've got some leftover mousse or pastry crème you can use it to change up the flavour of the filling.

Here's your chance to explore your creativity with a childhood favourite: chocolate-coated marshmallow biscuits (Wagon Wheels). The lollipop is fun and quirky: try serving it set in a little pot of greenery. Then there's the lamington crossover version, as well as an interactive dessert to DIY. Have fun, kids!

The red graffiti adds a splash of colour.

Note: use food-grade lollipop sticks for these sweets.

MAKES 15

---

100 g (3½ oz) smooth peanut butter
50 g (1¾ oz) raspberry jam
150 g (5½ oz) dark chocolate
30 g (1 oz) cocoa butter (optional)

SABLE BISCUIT
75 g (2¾ oz) unsalted butter
50 g (1¾ oz) icing (confectioners') sugar
1 egg
150 g (5 oz/1 cup) plain (all-purpose) flour, sifted
½ vanilla bean, seeds scraped

RASPBERRY MARSHMALLOW
6 sheets titanium-strength gelatine, softened in
     cold water
40 ml (1¼ fl oz) glucose syrup (see glossary)
30 ml (1 fl oz) raspberry purée (see glossary)
½ vanilla bean, seeds scraped
160 g (5¾ oz) caster (superfine) sugar

RED GRAFFITI (OPTIONAL)
50 g (1¾ oz) cocoa butter
10 g (⅜ oz) titanium white colour
5 g (⅛ oz) red colour

To make the sable, preheat the oven to 160°C (315°F).
Line a baking tray with baking paper.

Put the butter and icing sugar in the bowl of an
electric mixer fitted with the paddle attachment.
Starting on low speed, then increasing to medium
speed, beat until pale and creamy. Continue beating
as you add the egg. Gradually add the flour and the
vanilla seeds and mix until a smooth dough forms.

Shape the dough into a flat rectangle, then wrap
in plastic wrap and refrigerate for at least 4 hours.

On a floured surface, roll the chilled dough out
to 5 mm (¼ inch) thick. Use a 4 cm (1½ inch) round
cookie cutter to cut out 30 discs.

Lay the discs on the prepared baking tray and
bake for 15–20 minutes until golden. Cool on the tray
then set aside in an airtight container until needed.

To make the marshmallow, put the softened
gelatine and the glucose syrup in the bowl of an
electric mixer fitted with the whisk attachment.

Combine 100 ml (3½ fl oz) of water in a saucepan
with the raspberry purée, vanilla bean and seeds
and the sugar. Bring to the boil.

Pour the boiling liquid into the mixing bowl with
the gelatine mixture and start whisking on low
speed. Increase to high speed for about 3–5 minutes
until the marshmallow has cooled (make sure it's still
slightly warm when you work with it, once it sets it
will be hard to push into shape).

Lay 15 of the sable discs on a tray lined with
baking paper and then place a food-grade lollipop
stick in the middle of each disc.

Put the peanut butter in a piping (icing) bag fitted
with a small nozzle and pipe the peanut butter in a
circular motion onto the sable, working from the
outside in and leaving a 1 cm (⅜ inch) gap in the
centre. Place a dollop of raspberry jam in the gap.

Put the marshmallow in a piping (icing) bag
and pipe the marshmallow into the middle of each
sable disc.

Lay the remaining sable discs on top and press
down carefully so that the marshmallow reaches
the edge. Transfer to the refrigerator until set.

To complete the lollipops, Melt the chocolate
and cocoa butter in a microwave-proof bowl (see
page 232) until about two-thirds of the chocolate has
melted. Stir the chocolate until completely smooth
and cooled down to 29°C (84°F) using a thermometer.

Holding the lollipop stick, dip the lollipops in the
melted chocolate. Allow excess chocolate to drip off,
then place on a tray lined with baking paper or
acetate. Transfer to the refrigerator until the
chocolate has set.

To decorate, melt the cocoa butter in a
microwave, add the titanium colouring and blitz
with a handheld blender to combine. Add the red
colouring and blitz to combine. Pass through a fine
sieve and cool to 34°C (93°F) or just below body
temperature. Use a clean, dry pastry brush to flick
the graffiti onto the lollipops.

This creation is similar to a chocolate fondue, where the different elements are presented on a dish and the guests assemble their own dessert. It's fun and interactive.

SERVES 5

30 sable biscuits (see page 225)
100 g (3½ oz) smooth peanut butter
150 g (5½ oz) raspberries, halved
250 g (9 oz) milk chocolate, melted

VANILLA MARSHMALLOW
80 g (2¾ oz) caster (superfine) sugar
1 vanilla bean, seeds scraped
3 sheets titanium-strength gelatine, softened in cold water
1 tablespoon glucose syrup
50 g (1¾ oz) nonmelting icing (confectioners') sugar

To make the marshmallow, put 50 ml (1¾ fl oz) of water in a small saucepan with the caster sugar and vanilla seeds and bring it to the boil.

Meanwhile, put the softened gelatine and glucose in the bowl of an electric mixer fitted with the whisk attachment.

When the saucepan starts to boil, turn the electric mixer on to medium speed and slowly pour in the boiling syrup. Increase to high speed and whisk the marshmallow until warm.

Meanwhile, line a 10 x 15 cm (4 x 6 inch) container with plastic wrap and spray with baking spray.

Pour the warm marshmallow into the tin and spread it out evenly with a palette knife. Lightly spray the top of the marshmallow with baking spray and lay a piece of plastic wrap on top. Set at room temperature for at least 2–3 hours.

When ready to serve, remove the marshmallow from the tin and use a knife sprayed with baking spray to cut it into 3 cm (1¼ inch) cubes. Dust each cube with non-melting icing sugar. Arrange marshmallows in a tall glass bowl.

Put the peanut butter, raspberries and melted chocolate into individual bowls and arrange on a serving platter with a stack of sable biscuits.

3SOME TWIST
Make S'mores by placing a marshmallow and jam between two sable biscuits and microwave for 15 seconds to make it gooey.

This is a cool **date-night activity.** It's fun, **a bit romantic** and it can get quite **messy as well.**

Lamington gets a facelift, the sponge replaced with sable biscuit to add crunch. These go out like hot cakes... for events, gifts and that perfectly naughty sweet treat!

MAKES 15

100 g (3½ oz) raspberry jam
200 g (7 oz) dark chocolate
20 g (¾ oz) cocoa butter (optional)
150 g (5½ oz) shredded (desiccated) coconut

SABLE BISCUIT
75 g (2¼ oz) unsalted butter
50 g (1¾ oz) icing (confectioners') sugar
1 egg
100 g (3½ oz/⅔ cup) plain (all-purpose) flour, sifted
50 g (1¾ oz) cocoa powder (unsweetened)
½ vanilla bean, seeds scraped

MARSHMALLOW
160 g (5¾ oz) caster (superfine) sugar
½ vanilla bean, seeds scraped
6 sheets titanium-strength gelatine, softened in cold water
2 tablespoons glucose syrup

To make the sable, preheat the oven to 160°C (315°F). Line a baking tray with baking paper.

Put the butter and icing sugar in the bowl of an electric mixer fitted with the paddle attachment. Starting on low speed, then increasing to medium speed, beat until pale and creamy.

Continue beating as you add the egg. Gradually add the flour, cocoa and the vanilla seeds and mix until a smooth dough forms.

Gather the dough into a ball, shape into a flat rectangle, then wrap in plastic wrap and refrigerate for at least 4 hours.

On a floured surface, roll the chilled dough out to 5 mm (¼ inch) thickness. Use a 5 cm (1½ inch) diameter cookie cutter to cut the dough into 30 discs.

Lay the discs on the prepared baking tray and bake for 15–20 minutes until golden. Cool on the tray then set aside in an airtight container until ready to use.

To make the marshmallow, combine 100 ml (3½ fl oz) of water in a saucepan with the sugar and vanilla seeds. Bring to the boil.

Meanwhile, put the softened gelatine and the glucose syrup in the bowl of an electric mixer fitted with the whisk attachment.

Turn the mixer onto medium speed and pour the boiling liquid into the mixing bowl with the gelatine mixture. Increase to high speed for about 3–5 minutes until the marshmallow has cooled (make sure it's still slightly warm when you work with it, once it sets it will be hard to push into shape).

Lay 15 of the sable discs on a tray lined with baking paper and place a 1 cm (⅜ inch) dollop of raspberry jam in the centre of each disc.

Put the marshmallow into a piping (icing) bag fitted with a size 10 nozzle. Pipe the marshmallow into the middle of each sable disc in a dollop about 2 cm (¾ inch) high.

Place the remaining sable discs on top of the marshmallow and carefully press down so that the marshmallow reaches the edge of the sable. Transfer to the refrigerator until the marshmallow has set.

Put the milk chocolate and cocoa butter, if using, in a small microwave-proof bowl and melt in the microwave until two-thirds of the chocolate is melted. Stir the chocolate until completely smooth and cooled down to 29°C (84°F).

Use a fork to dip the marshmallow biscuits into the melted chocolate, making sure the entire surface is covered. Allow excess chocolate to drip off, then place on a tray lined with baking paper or acetate.

Cover one side of the Wag-Annas with shredded coconut and transfer to the refrigerator to set.

3SOME TWIST
The shelf life of the Wag-Annas, once dipped into chocolate, is about one day before the chocolate starts cracking and the biscuit starts to soften: you really need to be eating it with a crunch.

This is a list of some specialist equipment and ingredients you will need to make many of the recipes in this book. You will find many of these at specialty cake decorating and kitchen supply stores.

Acetate sheets: Clear, flexible plastic sheets used for setting tempered chocolate to help achieve a smooth finish.

Anglaise, crème anglaise: This is another name for a custard: a combination of milk, sugar and eggs cooked to a thick consistency.

Baking spray: Non-stick spray for easy application to baking sheets, tins and mats.

Cacao nibs: Chips of unprocessed cacao beans, available from gourmet food stores and chocolate suppliers.

Cartouche: A disc of heavy paper such as baking paper that covers a liquid to prevent a skin forming as the liquid cools.

Chocolate: There are three main types of chocolate: white chocolate, made with cocoa butter; dark chocolate, with 54% or more cocoa solids; and milk chocolate. When the chocolate has a name, such as Alunga or Venezuela, it is referring to a particular region or type of cacao bean that has qualities that suit the recipe. If you can't find the exact type, choose a chocolate with a similar percentage of cocoa. See also instructions for tempering chocolate on page 232.

Chocolate transfer sheet: Paper printed with edible designs that can be transferred onto tempered chocolate as decoration. The Firecracker design was printed especially for Anna; if you can't find a similar design, try any brightly coloured pattern.

Crème pâtissiere: A thick sweet custard cream often used for filling pastry.

Crèmeux: French for 'creamy', this name is given to an anglaise that is taken a step further, usually with the addition of gelatine for stability.

Cutters, round: You'll need a set of round biscuit or scone cutters from about 2.5 cm (1 inch) and up, as well as some specialty shapes, such as the ninja cutters for the Ginger Ninjas on page 179.

Electric mixer with whisk, dough hook and paddle attachments: One of these machines will save your arm muscles!

Flour, strong: Strong flour is also known as bread flour and is a high-gluten form of wheat flour that is good for breadmaking and other recipes where the gluten is essential to getting the desired finish.

Freezer film: Also known as Go-Betweens, this thin plastic is generally sold as a separating layer for placing between flat items in the freezer. I use it a lot to cover hot liquids and prevent a skin forming.

Gelatine, titanium-strength: The recipes in this book use titanium-strength gelatine sheets as a setting agent. Each sheet weighs 5 g (⅙ oz) and sets 250 ml (9 fl oz/1 cup) of liquid to a firm jelly. Soak sheets of gelatine in cold water to soften. To use, gently squeeze to remove excess water, then stir the softened sheets into the mixture you want to set.

Glucose syrup: Also known as corn syrup, this is a liquid sweetening agent.

Grué: From the French for cacao nibs, grué is a crunchy chocolate filling.

Hazelnut praline paste: Made by caramelising roasted hazelnuts in sugar and then grinding them to a paste, you can buy this paste ready-made or make it yourself.

Hulling strawberries: To remove the green leafy part of a strawberry without cutting the fruit, grasp the leaves between your fingers and twist, pulling away from the strawberry.

Icing (confectioners') sugar, non-melting: Also known as Snow Sugar, this type of icing sugar won't dissolve on contact with warm or moist surfaces, so it is great for a lasting finish on your desserts.

Junket tablet: Cheese is made by separating milk into curds and whey (remember the old nursery rhyme?) using rennet, which contains enzymes. Junket tablets contain rennet and are available in supermarkets.

Mango pearls: Mango-flavoured jelly (gelatine) balls: purchase these from bubble tea shops.

Microwave-proof bowls: I always melt chocolate in a microwave, as I believe it gives you better control over the temperature of the chocolate. See the instructions for tempering chocolate on page 232.

Milk, unhomogenised: Homogenised means the cream has been blended into the milk. In unhomogenised milk, the cream often forms a layer on top of the liquid. For cheese-making, this type of milk is best.

Nappage: Nappage is a transparent glaze that is often made of diluted apricot jam (jelly) and is available ready-made. It prevents fruit and other ingredients from drying out or browning and adds a glossy finish. You can also make your own using the BRUSH ME PRETTY recipe on page 232.

Oranges, segmenting: To segment oranges, use a small sharp knife to carefully remove the white pith and membrane and set the peeled segments aside in a shallow bowl until ready to use.

Pailleté feuilletine: Also called crepes dentelles, these are a light biscuit crumble made from extremely thin crisp pancakes crushed into small flakes.

Palette knife, offset (or crank-handled): A palette knife is a flat metal blade that is thin enough to slide underneath pastries and chocolates to lift them. They are also used to spread chocolate and anglaise and achieve a smooth finish on icing. An offset palette knife has a bend in the end of the blade near the handle that allows it to get into tricky angles.

Pectin: Derived from apples, this is a setting agent used in jams and jellies. The difference between pectin NH and yellow pectin is that yellow pectin sets solid, while pectin NH forms a softer, malleable gel.

Pipettes: Small plastic tubes with a squeezable bulb on the end, these are used for dispensing small amounts of liquids and gels. These are available from cake decorating supply stores or kitchen supply stores.

Piping (icing) bag and nozzles of various shapes and sizes: You can get disposable piping bags, or even make your own by twisting a cone of baking paper and securing it with masking tape. Some nozzles are plain, some are star or cross shaped and the St Honore nozzle is a long slit for dispensing waves of meringue or cream.

Popping candy: Carbonated candy, also known as Pop Rocks, that give the sensation of tiny explosions in the mouth. This is available from cake decorating and party supply stores.

Purée: To make fruit purée, simply process peeled and deseeded fruit in a blender or food processor until smooth or press it through a sieve. Store the purée in an airtight container in the refrigerator or freezer until it is needed. For passionfruit purée, cut the fruit in half and scoop the pulp and seeds into a small bowl, then stir to break up the fibres. If you want to remove the seeds, strain the pulp through a sieve.

Quenelle: Form a quenelle of mousse, sorbet or similar soft desserts by using a dessertspoon to pat the mousse into an almond shape.

Sable basque: A biscuitlike base or skirt for desserts.

Silicone mats and moulds: These flexible moulds have the benefit of going from oven to freezer without losing their shape or effectiveness. Set them on a baking tray for support.

Sorbet stabiliser: Improves the texture by minimising the size of ice crystals in sorbet. Available from specialty food stores.

Stainless steel bowls: Some recipes specify stainless steel bowls. These do not retain oils or odours and also make it easy to remove moulded desserts in one piece.

Sugar thermometer: When working with custards, chocolate and jelly (gelatine) it can be important to accurately measure temperatures. A sugar thermometer can be heated in a saucepan on the stovetop to quite high temperatures and is an inexpensive but important tool for dessertmaking.

Trimoline: This is another name for invert sugar: a syrup made by adding acid to simple sugar. It retains moisture and doesn't crystallise, so it's useful in baking and also in ice creams and sorbets.

Whipped cream siphon: This is a gas-charged bottle that adds air (usually nitrous oxide) to whipped cream as it is dispensed through the nozzle.

These basic recipes are used all the time by pastry chefs, as well as throughout this book. Once you've mastered them, try combining them in different ways to make your own creations!

PUMP UP... THE JAM

Pumped-up jam goes magically with Butter My Scones (see page 209) and can be mixed into ice cream, muffin mixes and even sweet dough.

———

MAKES 1 KG (2 LB 4 OZ)

———

600 g (1 lb 5 oz) frozen mixed berries
50 ml (1¼ fl oz) lemon juice
500 g (1 lb 2 oz) caster (superfine) sugar
2 teaspoons Pectin 325 NH (see glossary)
3 vanilla beans, split and seeds scraped
20 g (¾ oz) rose petals, edible

———

In a medium saucepan over low heat, combine the berries and lemon juice and cook for 15–20 minutes, until soft and the juices have come out. Make sure to stir every so often so that the berries do not catch.

Gradually stir in the 400 g (14 oz) of the caster sugar and reduce to low heat and bring to the boil. Remove from the heat.

Mix together the pectin and remaining caster sugar and stir it into the berry mixture.

Return the saucepan to low heat and bring to the boil. Add the vanilla beans and seeds.

Test the jam by placing a teaspoonful onto a dish and chilling it in the refrigerator. The jam should have a little bit of a run, but also stability to it. Remove from the heat, discard the vanilla beans and fold the rose petals through.

Transfer the jam to a clean, airtight container. It will keep for up to 4 weeks; if you use a sterilised jar, it will keep for a lot longer.

BRUSH ME PRETTY

Fruit glaze, which the French call nappage, helps prevent fresh fruit from softening and browning on a dessert. This recipe has a fruity taste, instead of the usual apricot glaze, and offers extra shine.

———

MAKES ABOUT 500 ML (17 FL OZ/2 CUPS)

———

200 g (7 oz) caster (superfine) sugar
1 vanilla bean, split and seeds scraped
peel of 1 lemon
peel of 1 orange
3 mint sprigs
3 teaspoons Pectin 325 NH (see glossary)
2 teaspoons lemon juice

———

Combine 500 ml (17 fl oz/2 cups) water, 150 g (5½ oz) of the caster sugar, the vanilla bean and seeds, and the lemon and orange peels in a small saucepan.

Bring to the boil over medium heat, then remove from the heat and add the mint. Set aside to infuse for 15 minutes.

Combine the pectin and the remaining sugar in a small bowl. Set aside.

Discard the mint sprigs, return the saucepan to medium heat and bring back to the boil. Remove from the heat and stir in the pectin mixture. Return to the boil for a further 10 minutes.

Test the consistency of the nappage by putting a teaspoonful on a dish and chilling it in the refrigerator. You want a thick liquid that holds its shape and doesn't run.

Stir in the lemon juice and strain though a fine sieve into a clean container.

Use straight away or cover the surface with plastic wrap and store in the refrigerator for 3–4 weeks.

Warm in the microwave when you want to use it. If it's still too thick, add a little water. Make sure not to double-dip your brush in the storage container.

VANILLA PASTRY CRÈME

Vanilla pastry crème is a thick vanilla custard that you'll use throughout this book. It is one of my favourite recipes.

___

MAKES 550 G (1 LB 4 OZ)

___

500 ml (17 fl oz/2 cups) milk
1 vanilla bean, split and seeds scraped
7 egg yolks
125 g (4½ oz) caster (superfine) sugar
50 g (1¾ oz/⅓ cup) custard powder, or cornflour (cornstarch)
50 g (1¾ oz) unsalted butter, at room temperature

___

Combine the milk with the vanilla bean and seeds in a medium heavy-based saucepan over medium heat. Bring to the boil.

Meanwhile, whisk together the egg yolks and sugar in a medium heatproof bowl until well combined. Add the custard powder and whisk well.

Pour a quarter of the hot milk mixture into the egg mixture. Stir well to combine.

Put the egg mixture into the saucepan with the remaining milk mixture over low heat. Slowly bring to a boil, stirring constantly so the eggs don't curdle or scorch on the bottom. When the mixture comes to a boil and thickens, continue to whisk to cook for 3–5 minutes or use a thermometer to indicate when the pastry cream reaches 85°C (185°F). Remove from the heat.

Pour the pastry cream into a stainless steel bowl. Cool to around 40°C (105°F), or just above body temperature.

Use a handheld blender to beat in the butter until well combined. Lay plastic wrap on the surface to prevent a skin forming chill in the refrigerator.

Use this as a filling for choux buns or layer it in millefeuille. You can also add flavours such as chocolate or matcha.

TEMPERING CHOCOLATE

Tempering chocolate gives it a glossy, smooth finish and makes it more stable to work with when making chocolate decorations for desserts. Once the chocolate is tempered, use a palette knife to spread it thinly on a sheet of acetate, or work it as instructed in the recipes in this book. It's got gloss, shine and snap.

___

DARK CHOCOLATE
Melt the chocolate in a microwave-proof bowl, in 40-second bursts, stirring between each burst until three-quarters of the chocolate is melted and smooth. Continue to stir the chocolate until it is completely melted and the temperature reaches 31–32°C (88–90°F).

___

MILK CHOCOLATE
Melt the chocolate in a microwave-proof bowl, in 30-second bursts, stirring between each burst until three-quarters of the chocolate is melted and smooth. Continue to stir the chocolate until it is completely melted and the temperature reaches 30–31°C (86–88°F).

___

WHITE CHOCOLATE AND FLAVOURED CHOCOLATE
Melt the chocolate in a microwave-proof bowl, in 40-second bursts, stirring between each burst until three-quarters of the chocolate is melted and smooth. Continue to stir the chocolate until it is completely melted and the temperature reaches 28–30°C (82–86°F).

We come across endless people that influence our lives, and I'm a true believer in surrounding ourselves with people who inspire, influence and direct us to be who we wish to be. So I thank the following people who have helped me through my book creation and construction of my success.

———————

Justine May, my manager and beyond that, more like my family. I love you endlessly with the utmost respect and I thank you for being there when we started, for now and for where we will go. Thanks too to Gary Mehigan for introducing us.

———————

Shangri-La Hotel, Sydney, for allowing all walls and obstacles to be removed to allow me to grow as a chef, as an individual and also to grow my brand too. Maybe I didn't fit the correct profile of a hotel chef, but the hotel saw beyond that. I'm very honoured and proud.

———————

Nikki To and Rhianne Contreras, the photography and styling team behind the book: we might have had long days but they were fun days.... Nikki, our 10-year friendship means we planned this a long time ago and I wouldn't have any other photographer shoot my cookbook but you. Rhianne, I have now adopted you as my food stylist. Thanks for no napkins.

———————

Felicity Goodchild, my right-hand woman, my assistant and my very good friend. You have been there from day one; I admire your hard work, determination and that you are constantly pushing me. Thank you for working so hard on my book with me, and being part of my success.

———————

Julie Sharp, you have been my mentor. My skill and imagination has a lot to do with you moulding me from the beginning. I am very blessed to know such a beautiful and supportive person.

———————

My team, the past, current and future. All success is accomplished due to one team with many dreams. A special thank you to my sous chef Edith Verboomen for holding the fort whilst I went out to create this book. Thanks also to Mikayla Brightling, Ashleigh Strauss and Sean Gao-Jie Hu for your help.

———————

Murdoch Books, thank you for your patience over the long process of making this book. Corinne Roberts, Hugh Ford and Melody Lord. What a collaboration! I choose to work with the best to create the best book for me and my fans.

———————

My mother, Eugina Polyviou — who never minded what I did as long as it was an honest job — for guiding me to the right direction, for her words of wisdom, for making me go to Greek school and teaching me about our heritage, and being proud.

———————

Endemol Shine for allowing me to shine and kickstarting me to become a TV star, which has opened so many doors. Gary Willis, my chocolate daddy, forever supporting me from day one. Kenwood for having me as your ambassador.

———————

Last of all my fans, from all around the world. This book was finally finished due to you guys and I am very humbled to be loved, adored, and accepted for just being me. I hope that this book inspires you all, as you guys inspire me to keep striving.

———————

Published in 2018 by Murdoch Books, an imprint of Allen & Unwin

Murdoch Books Australia
83 Alexander Street
Crows Nest NSW 2065
Phone: +61 (0) 2 8425 0100
murdochbooks.com.au
info@murdochbooks.com.au

Murdoch Books UK
Ormond House
26–27 Boswell Street
London WC1N 3JZ
Phone: +44 (0) 20 8785 5995
murdochbooks.co.uk
info@murdochbooks.co.uk

For Corporate Orders & Custom Publishing, contact our Business Development Team
at salesenquiries@murdochbooks.com.au.

Publisher: Corinne Roberts
Editorial Managers: Katie Bosher and Julie Mazur Tribe
Design: Hugh Ford
Project Editor: Melody Lord
Food Editor: Ross Dobson
Photographer: Nikki To
Stylist: Rhianne Contreras
Production Director: Lou Playfair

A cataloguing-in-publication entry is available from the catalogue of the
National Library of Australia at nla.gov.au.

ISBN 978 1 74336 769 8 Australia
ISBN 978 1 74336 818 3 UK

A catalogue record for this book is available from the British Library.

Colour reproduction by Splitting Image Colour Studio Pty Ltd, Clayton, Victoria
Printed by Hang Tai Printing Company Limited, China

The publisher and stylist would like to thank the following:
Luke Kennedy (@mynameislk), Neon Poodle (@neonpoodle),
Salt&Pepper (@saltandpepperhome), Seletti (@seletti_australia)
and Hayden Youlley Design (@haydenyoulley).

OVEN GUIDE: You may find cooking times vary depending on the oven you are using. For fan-forced ovens, as a general rule, set the oven temperature to 20°C (70°F) lower than indicated in the recipe.

MEASURES GUIDE: We have used 20 ml (4 teaspoon) tablespoon measures. If you are using a 15 ml (3 teaspoon) tablespoon add an extra teaspoon of the ingredient for each tablespoon specified.